BEA TOMS RECIPES

From A Country Cook

Book design by Dick Markey

ISBN: 0-9661278-7-0

PUBLISHED BY DIVERSIONS PUBLISHERS
FREDERICK, MARYLAND

Printed in the United States

DEDICATION

With heartfelt thanks I dedicate this book
to my family, and to all of those folks
who have appreciated my efforts over the years,
many of whom I am happy to call Friend.
It has been a wonderful journey.
A special thanks to Barbara Stull who typed this manuscript,
and also Richard Lebherz and Richard Markey
and other special friends
who have been so supportive and helpful
in making my books a reality.

FOREWORD

I have been cooking most of my eighty-eight plus years; from the time I was twelve years old, until the present time. I am still actively engaged in preparing foods for bridal showers, luncheons, christenings, birthday and anniversary parties, picnics and other family functions.

Over the years I have been asked for my recipes and urged to compile them into a cookbook. I feel it is now time to share them with my many friends and anyone who might wish to have them.

Many of my recipes date back to the 1930's and before. Early in my life I lived with a farm family in Frederick County, Maryland. I assisted with the farm chores, and also the cooking. There were always the daily meals to prepare, cooking for butcherings, holiday preparations, and feeding the threshing hands at harvest time. The men worked hard and had large and appreciative appetites. I learned to cook in large quantities, by necessity, on many of these occasions.

At eighteen and one half years, I married my husband, Clarke Toms in 1932. We had been classmates in high school. For a time we lived with his parents on the family farm. My husband's mother, (we were calling her "Grandma" fifteen months later), Grandma Toms, was a good and generous cook, having reared nine children. My husband was her youngest child. Some of my cooking knowledge, I attribute to her expertise and culinary skills, for everything was made from "scratch". On Saturdays, we prepared extra foods, baked pies and cakes in case "company" might drop in on Sunday. Oft times we might invite someone from church to come home with us, or family members or friends might just drop by in the afternoon. There were no fast-food stores or markets to which we might rush in case of an emergency. Friends and families visited one another more back then, after all, there was no television, or football games and country folk were not too well informed about the game of golf.

Several years later we were farming a large dairy farm in Montgomery County, Maryland. A very prominent doctor owned it. I took care of his aged, invalid mother. Frequently I prepared the food and served dinner parties for him and his fellow doctors and other guests. It was quite a challenge for me, but his guests seemed to enjoy and appreciate my foods. It was a great inspiration to me, country cook that I was.

My oldest daughter, Joan, was married while we were there. I prepared the food for her wedding reception, which was held in the doctor's home, in which we lived. People began asking for my recipes and the foods that I had prepared.

Ultimately, we moved to a farm we had purchased in Frederick County, Maryland. Our second daughter, Patricia, was married there, and again, I prepared the food for the wedding reception. Guests again were asking for my recipes and prepared foods and that's how it all began. I didn't start going out to serve parties until 1966, but that's another whole story.

My cookbook contains, for the most part, recipes I have created using a little of this and a little of that and some imagination. Many recipes, I have adjusted or amended to suit the times and circumstances. Most of the recipes are the result of experimentation and concentration on taste and eye appeal.

Other recipes I have received from family members and friends over these many years, some dating back some sixty to seventy years; for example, my Slumgullion Stew, which I remember from my early childhood home. The picture of it simmering on the stove is still vivid in my mind. I have created the recipe from the mental picture of the ingredients and the aroma of it cooking, still in my mind.

My daughter, Patricia, first gave my roll recipe to me some thirty or thirty five years ago. She was a Home Economics teacher at the time. I doubt she would recognize the recipe as it now reads. The same would be true of Grandma Toms' recipe for "Old Fashioned Sugar Cookies".

The most difficult part of putting the book recipes together was reducing and defining the proper quantities of the various ingredients, as I had for years prepared the recipes in much larger quantities. I have tried to keep the recipes relatively simple and easy to prepare. I do hope you will enjoy preparing the foods and that you and your family will find the dishes tasty and to your liking.

My profound thanks to you and to those of you who have permitted me to share in the happy and special times in the lives of so many of your families. I assure you it has been a very special privilege. Through the years so many have accepted my efforts and made me very happy to feel that, even at my age, I still have something to offer. You have given me a very special gift. Thank you, thank you.

Beatrice Toms

Contents

Appetizers

CHEESE STRAWS
MAKES ABOUT 100 STICKS

1 8-oz. package extra sharp cheddar cheese
1½ cups all-purpose flour
1½ sticks butter or margarine
¼ cup grated Parmesan cheese
⅓ teaspoon garlic salt
⅓ teaspoon paprika

Grate extra sharp cheese (very fine), sift flour, garlic salt and paprika together. Beat butter or margarine and extra sharp cheese together until smooth. Add Parmesan cheese and mix well. Slowly add flour until well mixed. Scrape side and bottom of mixing bowl to be sure all is well mixed. Put dough into cookie press (with star tip) and press onto ungreased cookie sheet. I press them into long rows about 1 inch apart. Bake at 350 degrees about 8 minutes. Don't over bake!

I cut them into about 2½ inch sticks when they are removed from the oven.

SHRIMP DIP
SERVES ABOUT 25 PEOPLE

13

2 cans (6.7-oz.) baby shrimp
½ lb. shredded cheddar cheese
1½ tablespoons minced onion or fresh onion
2-3 dashes Worcestershire sauce
1 cup good mayonnaise
1 teaspoon lemon juice
garlic salt to taste

Blend all together in mixing bowl.
Adjust seasonings to taste.
Serve with corn chips or other firm "diggers", or chips.
For hors d'oeuvres.

COCKTAIL MEAT BALLS
MAKES 75-80

14

2 pounds of good quality ground beef
½ cup finely minced onion
2 eggs
1 cup bread crumbs
½ teaspoon salt
1 tablespoon parsley flakes
1 (29-oz.) can good tomato sauce
garlic salt

Mix all the ingredients except the tomato sauce
and garlic salt together well.
Form into small balls.
Place in a rectangular baking pan about 2½" deep.
Sprinkle with garlic salt.
Cover with tomato sauce.
Bake uncovered in 300-325 degree oven
for about 30 minutes or until firm to the touch.
Serve hot in chafing dish.
These are also perfect to serve with cooked spaghetti.

HOT CRAB SPREAD
SERVES ABOUT 20

1 lb. fresh crab meat (back fin or regular, no claw meat)
2 (8-oz.) cream cheese (room temperature)
1 cup sour cream
3 tablespoons mayonnaise
1½ tablespoons lemon juice or cream sherry
dash Tabasco sauce (to taste)
¼ cup ketchup
1 tablespoon Worcestershire sauce
½ teaspoon dry mustard
3 shakes of garlic salt
1 cup shredded cheddar cheese
½ cup sliced almonds.

Pick over crab meat carefully to remove any cartilage
add ½ cup of the shredded cheese, set aside

Beat softened cream cheese in mixer, add sour cream, mayonnaise,
lemon juice, or sherry, Tabasco, ketchup, Worcestershire sauce,
dry mustard, and garlic salt to taste. Mix until well blended.
Add to crab and cheese. Spoon into casserole.
Cover with remaining shredded cheese.
Sprinkle almonds over casserole.
Bake uncovered in 325 degree oven about 30 minutes.
Or until set.
Serve hot as Hors d'oeuvres
with crackers or Melba toast on the side.
Double recipe for 3-quart casserole.

RUMAKI
YIELDS 20 APPETIZERS

10 slices bacon cut in half
10 chicken livers cut in half
10 medium water chestnuts halved
⅓ cup soy sauce
3 tablespoons light brown sugar
⅙ teaspoon ground ginger

Combine the soy sauce, brown sugar and ginger.
Mix until the sugar dissolves.
Drain chicken livers and cover them with the marinade.
Keep them in the marinade about 1 hour, turn them several times.
Drain them well. Lay the half slice of bacon on flat surface.
Place the half liver and half water chestnut
on each piece of bacon.
Wrap the pieces of bacon around the liver and water chestnut.
Secure it with a wooden pick. Place in a shallow baking pan
and bake at 375-400 degrees until the bacon is crisp.
Remove from pan and drain on paper towels.
Serve hot.

STUFFED MUSHROOM CAPS
YIELDS 60 CAPS

60 medium-sized mushrooms
1½ lbs. ground beef
¾ lbs. shredded sharp cheddar cheese
1 small onion finely minced
3 eggs slightly beaten
1 cup fine, dry bread crumbs
garlic, salt to taste
2 tablespoons parsley flakes

Wash mushrooms through several times.
Drain and remove stems.
Lightly salt caps, if desired, I do not find it necessary.
Grind stems. Mix together ground stems,
ground beef cheese, onion, eggs, bread crumbs,
garlic, salt to taste and parsley flakes.
Fill caps with stem, beef etc mixture.
Bake, covered with foil, in 325 degree to 350 degree oven until
done. Remove covering for the last 5 minutes.

Any left over meat mixture may be formed into patties
and fried slowly on each side, until done,
much as you would do a hamburger

TOAST POINTS OR MINI PIZZAS
YIELDS ABOUT 48 PIECES

18

12 slices of a square loaf of bread
1 ¼ lbs. shredded sharp cheddar cheese
1 tablespoon Worcestershire sauce
2 tablespoons onion flakes
½ cup sliced almonds
good mayonnaise
⅔ cup bacon bits

Trim crusts from bread.
Mix all the ingredients together.
Add and blend in enough mayonnaise to
make the mixture of a good spreading consistency.
Spread trimmed slices of bread fairly
generously, smoothly covering each slice of bread.
Cut each spread slice into quarters.
Place on waxed paper covered, jelly roll type pan.
Toast in moderate oven until bread is
crisp and spread fully melted.

Any left-over spread may be stored in refrigerator,
keeps well.

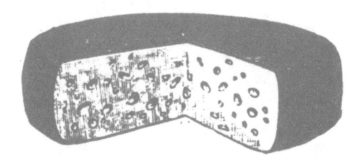

PINWHEEL PARTY SANDWICHES
1 LOAF MAKES ABOUT 75 SANDWICHES

1 loaf unsliced white bread
3 (8 oz.) packages cream cheese
½ cup pineapple or apricot preserves
red or green maraschino cherries
chopped pecans or English walnuts

Cut bread horizontally into about ¼ inch slices.
Trim the crusts from the bread.
Spread a slice of the bread with preserves spread.
Place a row of 4 or 5 cherries at one end of
the spread slice of bread and
roll up as you would a jelly roll.
Wrap roll in a piece of saran wrap.
Twist the wrap at each end of the
roll so the bread will not dry out.
Repeat with the other slices of bread.
Place in freezer to chill.
When firm, slice in ¼ inch slices.
Each roll will cut 8-9 slices
Rewrap and keep frozen until ready to serve.
The sandwiches can be made ahead and
kept frozen until ready to serve.
Put on tray just before serving.

Spread for Pinwheel and Ribbon Sandwiches
EACH RECIPE MAKES ABOUT 50-75 TEA-SIZE SANDWICHES

Fruit Spreads
3 (8-oz.) packages cream cheese
½ cup pineapple or apricot preserves
red or green maraschino cherries
chopped pecans or English walnuts

Deviled Ham Spread
3 (8-oz.) packages cream cheese
3 (4¼-oz.) cans deviled ham
small sweet round pickle
pickle relish or finely minced-sweet pickle

Tangy Cheese Spread
3 (8-oz.) packages cream cheese
1½ cups sharp cheese grated or
2 (5-oz.) jars Kraft Old English cheese spread
small stuffed green olives or
snipped ripe olives
bit of garlic
good on rye bread

The above recipes are for the spreads and
also the pickles, fruit and olives to enhance
and add interest to the various ribbon and pinwheel
type sandwiches.

PARTY STUFFED CELERY
MAKES 25-30 SERVINGS

25-30 (2½-inch) celery sticks
6 oz. cream cheese
1 (4½-oz.) can deviled ham
1½ tablespoons finely minced sweet pickle
paprika

In mixer blend beaten cream cheese,
deviled ham and pickles together.
Fill celery sticks.
Sprinkle very lightly with paprika.
Chill well.

PARTY CHEESE BALL
SERVES ABOUT 25 PEOPLE

2 (8-oz.) packages cream cheese
2 (5-oz. jars) Old English processed cheese
2 oz. blue cheese
4 oz. extra sharp cheddar cheese finely grated
scant tablespoon Worcestershire sauce
garlic salt to taste
1 cup finely minced pecans
1-2 maraschino cherries

Have all ingredients at room temperature.
Blend and mix cream cheese, grated extra sharp cheese, Old English cheese, and blue cheese. Beat well, add Worcestershire sauce, garlic salt and continue to beat until very smooth.
Adjust seasonings to taste. Line small bowl with saran wrap and spoon in cheese mixture, cover with saran wrap.
This will make one 2 pound ball or two 1 pound balls.
Refrigerate until firm.
Remove from bowl or 2 small containers and roll in pecans.
Top with maraschino cherry.
Keep refrigerated until ready to serve.
Serve with firm crackers on the side.

Wrap in saran wrap when refrigerated.

½ recipe will serve about 12 people.

CUCUMBER SANDWICHES
MAKES 30 SANDWICHES

23

30 (1¼ inch) rounds of white bread
1 firm fresh cucumber
8 oz. cream cheese
¾ teaspoon anchovy paste
¾ teaspoon lemon juice
¾ teaspoon onion flakes or grated fresh onion
garlic salt to taste

From a square loaf of white bread, cut 30 rounds
of bread with a 1½ inch cookie cutter.
Wash and dry cucumber. Score cucumber
lengthwise with a sharp pronged fork.
In mixer blend together cream cheese, + anchovy paste,
lemon juice, garlic salt and onion.
Adjust seasonings to taste. Slice cucumber.
Spread each round of bread with the cream cheese
and top with a cucumber slice.
Put the sandwiches in a flat container or
casserole dish and cover tightly.
Refrigerate.

If you wish you can shake a bit of paprika on the
cucumber sandwiches. I don't.

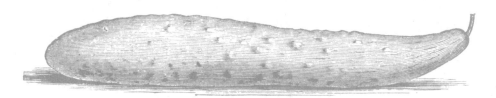

OPEN FACE RYE SANDWICHES
MAKES 30 SANDWICHES

*1 loaf of rye or pumpernickel bread or
party rye bread
1 (8-oz.) package cream cheese
1 (5-oz.) jar Old English processed cheese spread
15 stuffed olives cut in half
garlic salt to taste*

Mix cream cheese, processed cheese and garlic salt.
Cut 30 rounds of rye or pumpernickel bread.
Fill a pastry bag with cheese mix.
Use a large flower tip to make a rose on
each slice of bread. Top with ½ olive.

ON SANDWICHES

I hope you will find the sandwich recipes
I have submitted in this cook book helpful and enjoyable.
However, there are endless combinations of
ingredients that may be used in making good,
nutritious and delicious sandwiches.
Any kind of bread may be used; white, whole wheat,
cracked wheat, raisin, rye, pumpernickel, rolls, biscuits and so on.
Any kind of meats, seafood, chicken, cheese, eggs, fruits,
fresh vegetables, the list is endless.
Sandwiches are an excellent way to use left over roasts,
salad greens, cheese, fresh garden vegetables
in whatever combination you choose.
They can be served hot or cold, plain or toasted,
frozen ahead, covered with gravy or other sauces,
as with a hot roast beef sandwich.
The only real criteria is to use the foods
you and your family enjoy, and as with all
foods, season the way you like them.
Don't be afraid to experiment.

MARINATED MUSHROOMS
SERVES 4-6

12-15 large firm mushrooms
French dressing
finely minced green onions or chives
finely minced parsley

Wash mushrooms well and slice thinly.
Cover with French dressing.
Allow mushrooms to marinate in dressing for one hour or more.
Turn several times. Add minced onion or chives to mushrooms.
Serve on lettuce on a hot summer day.

A ham or cheese sandwich would make a nice lunch
with the mushrooms.

FRESH FRUIT TRAY
SERVES 25-30

½ of 1 seedless watermelon
1 honeydew melon
1 large or 2 small cantaloupes
1 fresh pineapple
fresh strawberries
grapes, red or white
kiwi or apple slices
leaf lettuce

Wash well and drain, enough leaf lettuce to cover tray.
Peel, slice and cube the melons.
Peel, core and slice pineapple into ½ inch slices
The pineapple can also be bought already peeled and cored.
Cut pineapple into cubes.
Cover a nice sized tray (round or rectangle) with
the leaf lettuce. Pat the lettuce dry with paper towels.
Place pineapple chunks in center of the tray.
Alternate the watermelon, honeydew, and cantaloupe
into wedges around the pineapple.
Kiwi or apple slices may be used to separate the melons.
Strawberries or small bunches of grapes are nice
to garnish the tray.
Use any fruit left over to refill tray.

SANDWICH FILLINGS
EACH RECIPE MAKES 3-4 CUPS

Chicken Salad Spread

2 cups ground or finely chopped, cooked chicken
1 cup finely chopped celery
2 tablespoons minced sweet pickle
mayonnaise to moisten

Ham Salad Spread

2 cups minced or ground cooked ham
½ cup minced celery
minced green peppers or sweet pickles
mayonnaise or French dressing to moisten

Beef Salad Spread

2 cups ground roast beef
½ cup minced celery
1 tablespoon minced chives or parsley
mayonnaise blended with 1 tablespoon horseradish to moisten

Egg Salad Spread

6 hard cooked eggs finely chopped
½ cup minced celery
minced sweet pickle or capers
¼ tablespoon mustard blended with
mayonnaise to moisten

Trim crusts from slices of bread (square loaf).
Spread filling on one slice of bread.
If spread is dry or too coarse I sometimes spread a
little mayonnaise or soft butter very thinly on top slice
so the sandwich will stick together better.
Cut sandwiches into 4 triangles or squares or other shapes.
Store in a covered container in refrigerator until served.

PARTY CHICKEN PUFFS
MAKES ABOUT 70 CHICKEN PUFFS

8 cups cooked chicken
4 cups finely minced celery
1 ⅓ cups finely minced sweet pickle
1 ¼ cups good mayonnaise

Chop chicken very fine, this should be very cold.
Add celery and sweet pickle, mix well.
Add mayonnaise and blend together.
Add a little more mayonnaise if you think it is necessary
Chill thoroughly.

Shells
8 extra large eggs
2 cups flour
2 sticks butter or margarine
½ teaspoon salt
2 ⅔ cups water

Break eggs into bowl.
Bring water and butter to a boil. Stir in flour and salt.
Beat vigorously and continue cooking until mixture
becomes a soft ball. Place in mixing bowl and beat,
add eggs one at a time, beating well after each addition.
Continue beating, scraping, mixture, from sides of bowl,
until mixture has a slight glaze.
Drop onto a lightly greased cookie sheet.
Using two teaspoons, dropping them much as you would
drop cookies. Bake in 400 degree oven about 30 minutes,
reduce temperature to 350 degrees and bake
another 5 minutes or until firm.
When cold, make a small opening in side of puff and
stuff with very cold chicken mixture.

Shells may also be used for cream puffs, ham salad,
shrimp salad, or crab salad or other fillings.

PUNCH
MAKES 16-18 ONE CUP SERVINGS

1 (2-quart can) pineapple juice
1 (2-quart bottle) ginger ale
1 pint orange juice
orange slices
halved strawberries (stems on)
ice cubes

Mix pineapple juice, ginger ale and orange juice together.
Garnish with orange slices.
For a pink punch omit orange juice and garnish with strawberries.
Add a little red food coloring to make a pink punch.
Serve chilled and add extra ice.

PARTY PUNCH
MAKES 16-18 ONE CUP SERVINGS

2 quart can pineapple juice
2 quart bottle ginger ale
1 quart vanilla ice cream
1 quart orange sherbet

Pour chilled ginger ale and pineapple juice over
the sherbet and ice cream.
Any other flavor sherbet may be used.
(Raspberry, lime or rainbow colored).
Serve very cold or add a few ice cubes if necessary.

Soups & Stews

31

SLUMGULLION (BEEF STEW)
MAKES ABOUT 5-6 SERVINGS

1½ lbs. cubed beef steak
4 tablespoons butter or margarine
1 cup finely minced onion
1 medium green pepper (diced)
1 minced clove of garlic or garlic powder
1½ cups fresh peeled or canned tomatoes
2 medium potatoes peeled and cubed
½ teaspoon oregano
2 cubes beef bullion or 1 tablespoon Worcestershire sauce
salt and pepper to taste

Cook potatoes in small amount of lightly salted water
until medium tender, set aside.
Dredge beef in small amount of seasoned flour (salt and pepper)
In a large skillet or sauce pan, melt butter or
margarine and sauté beef until lightly browned.
Add onion and garlic, sauté until tender.
Add peppers, sauté a few minutes.
Add the flour and stir until lightly browned
being careful not to let it burn.
Add tomatoes and mix all together.
Add a little water if necessary.
Cover and simmer about one hour or until beef is tender.
Check seasoning and adjust if necessary.
Add beef bullion cubes or Worcestershire sauce.
Add potatoes, and potato water, if needed.
Cover and simmer about 30 more minutes.
Serve hot.

A nice vegetable salad or hot biscuits or rolls
would be a nice accompaniment. Good, hearty, winter dish.

DELICIOUS CHICKEN CORN SOUP
SERVES 8-10

8 cups chicken broth
⅔ cup finely minced onion
2½ cups frozen, fresh, or canned corn
1 cup finely chopped celery
5 cups cooked, finely chopped chicken
1 cup home made (rivels, see table of contents)
finely minced parsley or parsley flakes
salt and pepper to taste

Bring chicken broth to boil, add celery, onion,
chopped chicken and corn and bring to boil again.
Add rivels to boiling soup and stir until rivels are nicely cooked.
Add extra chicken broth if necessary.
Allow soup to simmer until all ingredients are done.
Fine broken noodles may be used instead of the rivels.
In this case the soup should simmer
until they are well cooked.

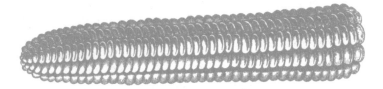

POTATO ONION SOUP
SERVES 5 OR 6

4 nice size potatoes
3 medium onions
3 cups water
2 teaspoons salt
1 stick butter or margarine
2 cups rich milk or 1 (13½-oz. can) evaporated milk
1 cup cubed, cooked, ham or 3 sliced frankfurters

Peel and dice potatoes and onions.
Cook potatoes and onions in salted water.
When potatoes are tender stir in ham
or sliced franks and milk and butter.
Add a little thickening to soup, if necessary

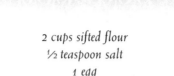

Rivel Soup
SERVES 6-8

35

2 cups sifted flour
½ teaspoon salt
1 egg
6-8 cups chicken, ham or beef broth

Combine flour, salt and egg.
Mix well until rivels are very fine. This can be done
by rubbing the mix between your two palms
or with the fine beater of your electric mixer.
Bring the chicken, ham or beef broth to a boil.
Add the rivels to the boiling liquid, stirring all the while,
so they will not stick together.
Cook about 10 minutes.

Minced onion, celery or any other vegetable
you might desire, may be added to the soup.
The rivels may also be added to
bean and potato soup to thicken it a bit.

Extra rivels may be stored in freezer for later use.

CHICKEN RICE SOUP
MAKES 10-12 MAIN DISH SERVINGS

6 cups chicken broth
5-6 cups finely cut cooked chicken
1 ½ cups finely cut celery
½ cup finely chopped onion
½ cup converted rice
½ cup good mayonnaise
2 tablespoons lemon juice
salt and pepper to taste
few parsley flakes (optional)

Add to the chicken broth the rice, celery,
onion, salt and pepper to taste.
Bring to boil and simmer until rice is done.
In a small bowl mix mayonnaise lemon juice,
and about ½ cup chicken broth until smooth.
Add slowly to chicken broth, etc. in pot. Stir well.
Add cut up chicken slowly, simmer about 15 to 20 minutes.
Add a little extra chicken broth or seasonings if necessary.
Add parsley flakes if desired.

Oyster Stew
SERVES 6-8

37

1 quart oysters
1 pint milk
1 pint half and half
½ teaspoon salt
⅛ teaspoon pepper
1 teaspoon onion juice
1 tablespoon minced parsley

Drain oysters and pour liquid into sauce pan.
Heat, do not boil. Heat milk and half and half in double boiler,
or over very low heat. Stir milk into oyster liquid.
Add butter and other seasonings to taste.
Add oysters last, when they begin to puff and
crinkle around the edges, sprinkle in
minced parsley and remove from the
heat and serve at once. Serve with tiny oyster crackers.

If you like the stew a little thicker blend
½ cup milk with 1½ tablespoon flour and add to hot
milk and oyster mixture, before adding oysters.

HEARTY BEEF VEGETABLE SOUP
MAKES 10-12 MAIN DISH SERVINGS

1½ lbs. stew beef (cut in ½ inch cubes)
4 tablespoons butter or margarine
12 cups water
salt and pepper
1½ cups fresh or frozen corn
2 cups of fresh or canned tomatoes
1 cup peeled and cubed potatoes
1 cup fresh or frozen cut green beans
1 cup diced carrots
1 cup baby lima beans
1 cup fresh or frozen green peas
1 cup chopped (fine) celery
1½ cups shredded cabbage
4 tablespoons minced onion
¾ cup pearled barley (optional)

Lightly sauté beef in butter or margarine.
Place in soup kettle and add salt, pepper and water.
Let beef and water simmer about an hour.
Add the vegetables, one at a time to the boiling broth
so it will keep simmering, add barley, cabbage and tomatoes last.
Simmer and taste periodically. Add salt or pepper to taste.
Add additional water as necessary.
Simmer until all ingredients are tender.

Any left over soup may be served at a later meal.
Omit any ingredient your family does not like,
or add any other ingredient they may like.
Always season to taste.

DUMPLINGS FOR SOUPS OR STEWS
MAKES 6-8 SMALL DUMPLINGS

39

1 cup all purpose flour
2 teaspoons baking powder
½ teaspoon salt
2 tablespoons snipped parsley
1 egg
¼ cup milk
2 tablespoons melted butter

Mix together flour, baking powder, and salt.
Add snipped parsley.
Stir together egg, milk and melted butter.
Combine flour mixture and egg mixture,
stirring just enough to blend them well.
Drop dough from tablespoon into boiling liquid.
Cover with tight lid at once.
Reduce heat to very low and allow the stew
or soup just to simmer about 12-15 minutes.
Do not lift the lid until they are done.

These dumplings are delightful with
most any thick soup or stew.
Chicken or beef stew, red kidney beans
or Great Northern bean soup, etc.

40

Casseroles

SUPER EGG CASSEROLE
SERVES 6-8

2 tablespoons butter or margarine
6 spring or green onions thinly sliced
12 eggs well beaten
1⅓ cups milk
¾ teaspoon seasoned salt
1½ cups diced mild ham
3 cups shredded cheddar cheese

42

Melt butter or margarine in skillet.
Sauté onions over medium to low heat until softened.
Add to onions, eggs, the milk, salt, diced ham and
2 cups of the shredded cheese.
Pour mixture into a buttered 2-quart casserole.
Bake uncovered in a 350 degree
oven about 30 minutes or until the eggs set.
Remove from the oven and sprinkle with the remaining cheese.
Return to oven a few minutes until the cheese melts.

Crumbled bacon may be used instead of the ham,
and one cup sliced mushrooms may be added.
In that case sauté the mushrooms with the green onions.

BEST EVER BAKED OMELET
SERVES 6

43

½ lb. lean sausage
8 beaten eggs
2-3 tablespoons fine minced onions
1 teaspoon chopped pimento
1 teaspoon salt
¼ teaspoon pepper
1 cup shredded cheddar cheese
1 cup shredded Swiss cheese
1 tablespoon flour
¾ cup milk

Sauté sausage in skillet until lightly browned.
Remove from heat and drain well. Set aside.
Reserve 1 tablespoon sausage drippings.
Sauté onions in the drippings until tender.
Add to the onions, the sausage, beaten eggs,
milk, pimento, parsley, salt and pepper.
Mix well
Combine the 2 cheeses and flour and add to the egg mixture.
Pour all into a 1½ - 2-quart buttered casserole.
Bake at 325 to 350 degrees about 40 minutes or until set.
Serve immediately.

* This is an excellent brunch dish.
You may also substitute 6 bacon slices for the sausage.
Sauté the bacon and crumble into small pieces
and proceed with the recipe the same as you
would with the sausage.

MASHED POTATO CASSEROLE
SERVES 8-10

9 medium baking potatoes
½ cup butter or margarine
⅔ cup hot milk
1 ½ cups shredded cheddar cheese
1 cup whipping cream
salt and pepper to taste

44

Peel and boil potatoes in lightly salted water,
drain and beat in mixing bowl until light and fluffy.
Add butter, salt and pepper to taste and
carefully beat in hot milk, a little at a time.
Check for seasoning, spread potatoes
smoothly put in buttered casserole dish.
Fold shredded cheddar cheese into whipped cream.
Spread whipped cream and cheddar cheese mix
evenly over top of casserole.
Bake in 350 degree oven 30-35 minutes
until a golden brown.

You may use a cup of beaten sour cream
instead of whipping cream if you prefer.

HUNGRY MAN CASSEROLE
SERVES 12-15

4 medium potatoes sliced or cubed and cooked
2 lbs. loose country sausage
1 lb. shredded cheddar cheese
6 eggs
2 cups milk
1 (20-oz.) can cream of mushroom soup
2 tablespoons flour
salt and pepper to taste (depends on sausage)
dash of Tabasco
¾ teaspoon dry mustard
½ cup finely minced onion or ⅓ cup onion flakes
½ cup water

Cook sliced or cubed potatoes in lightly salted water.
When almost done, drain well and set aside.
Sauté sausage until lightly browned.
Drain off most of fat.
Place potatoes in a 9 x 13 inch greased casserole dish.
Cover with shredded cheese,
then with the sausage.
Beat eggs and add slowly milk, flour, Tabasco,
dry mustard and onion and mix well.
Pour this mixture over the casserole.
Dilute mushroom soup with ½ cup water
and spread over the casserole.
Bake at 325 to 350 degrees for about 40 minutes.

Casserole can be made ahead, in that case cover with
mushroom soup just before baking and cover
with saran wrap or foil until ready to bake.

SPAGHETTI CASSEROLE
SERVES 6

46

8 oz. thin spaghetti
3 slices bacon, minced
¾ pound ground beef
3 tablespoons olive oil
½ cup finely minced onion
⅓ cup finely chopped green peppers
2½ cups canned tomatoes (chopped)
1 (4.5-oz) jar sliced mushrooms
salt and pepper to taste
Parmesan cheese

Cook, drain and rinse spaghetti according to package directions.
Sauté bacon until lightly browned, add beef and olive oil.
Cook and stir until beef is nearly done.
Add tomatoes and mushrooms, including their liquid in jar.
Stir and cook until well blended. Adjust seasonings if necessary.
Put ½ cooked spaghetti into greased round casserole.
Spoon ½ meat sauce over spaghetti. Add remaining spaghetti
and top with remainder of meat sauce.
Cover generously with Parmesan cheese.
Bake at 350 degrees for about ½ hour.

HOMINY SUPERB

SERVES 12-15

47

2 (29-oz.) cans cooked hominy
¾ lb. diced smoked (not country) ham
3 cups shredded cheddar cheese
1 stick butter, melted
3 tablespoons onion flakes
salt and pepper to taste
about 1½ cups water
buttered bread crumbs

Mix together first seven ingredients.
Add more water if necessary
Top with buttered bread crumbs.
Bake at 325 to 350 degrees until hominy
is good and tender, about 30 to 40 minutes.

Excellent brunch dish

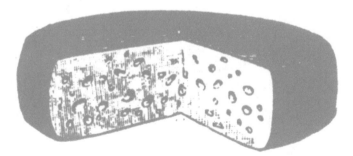

CHICKEN BEATRICE
SERVES 15

4 cups cooked and chopped chicken
1 cup uncooked rice
8-oz. can water chestnuts chopped
2 cups finely chopped celery
½ cup finely minced onion (fresh)
20-oz can cream of chicken soup
1⅓ cups mayonnaise
2 cups crushed corn flakes
4 oz melted butter
½ cup sliced almonds

Cook rice in 2½ cups water or chicken broth.
If in water add about 1 teaspoon of salt or some
chicken bullion and ⅓ stick of butter.
Bring rice to a boil, then cover and reduce
heat to low, to let the rice steam
slowly for about 20 minutes.
Stir often so as not to let the rice stick.
When rice is cooked and cooled a bit,
mix all the chicken, rice and the other ingredients together.
Transfer to a casserole, top with buttered corn
flakes, and sprinkle over with
the sliced almonds. Bake uncovered in 325 degree oven
for about 45 minutes or until it bubbles in the middle.

If it seems a little too stiff when mixed together add a little
water, milk, or chicken broth to mixture
before placing in casserole.

48

BAKED FRUIT COMPOTE
SERVES 12-15

1 (29-oz.) can peach halves
1 (29-oz). can pear halves
1 (29-oz.) can pineapple chunks
1 cup red maraschino cherries halved
4 tablespoons flour
1½ sticks butter or margarine
1½ cups light brown sugar
1½ cups cream sherry
1 jar spiced apple rings

49

Cut peaches and pears into small chunks.
Drain peaches, pears, pineapple and cherries.
Melt butter or margarine stir in slowly flour
and brown sugar. Continue stirring over medium heat.
Blend in sherry. Stir until it thickens. Put the fruit
mixture into large stainless pan or bowl.
Pour syrup over drained fruit. Let stand a
few hours or over night. Spoon mixture into
3-quart casserole, top with spiced apple rings.
Bake 325 degree oven for about 45 minutes or until
fruit and syrup are nice and bubbly.
Serve warm.

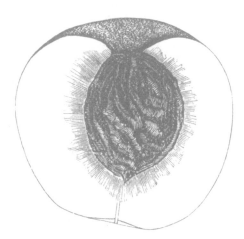

Baked Hash and Potatoes
SERVES 6

1 cup left over gravy or make a gravy
1 cup cooked and diced potatoes
⅓ cup minced onion
⅓ cup chopped green pepper
salt to taste
1 teaspoon Worcestershire sauce
2½ tablespoons chopped pimentos
2 cups diced precooked ham
½ cup tomato puree or fresh crushed tomatoes
½ cup buttered bread crumbs
½ cup shredded cheddar cheese

Use left over gravy or use the following recipe for the gravy.
Melt 2 tablespoons butter, when hot stir in 2 tablespoons flour,
sautéed onion, then stir in a cup of water and
dissolved beef cube.
Stir until blended well add salt if necessary
and Worcestershire sauce.
Add the potatoes, green peppers, minced pimentos,
ham and tomato puree. Mix well.
Pour into 1½ or 2-quart casserole.
Cover with shredded cheese and top with buttered crumbs.
Bake in 350 degree oven until cooked through well and
lightly browned about 35-40 minutes.

You may substitute beef or other meat for the ham.
This is a hearty dish.

BAKED APPLES
SERVES 6

6 baking apples
sugar
raisins
butter
cinnamon
water

Wash and cut apples in half (stem to bottom).
Remove the core. Place in baking dish.
Sprinkle generously with sugar about 1 to 1½ tablespoons
per apple depending on tartness of the apples.
Place a small pat of butter in each half apple.
Sprinkle on seedless raisins as generously as you like
and shake a little cinnamon over the top of all the apples.
Add about one tablespoon of water for each apple half.
Bake in moderate oven 350 degrees until done.
Test with pick about 20-30 minutes should be long enough.
They may be baked whole if desired.
Add nuts if you like.

STEAMED RICE
SERVES 6-8

2 cups long grained rice
5 cups water or chicken broth
2 teaspoons salt if cooking with water
1 stick of butter or margarine

Bring rice and water to a boil, cut heat back
to very low heat, cover, and let steam
slowly about ½ hour or until done.
Stir to avoid sticking. Add water if necessary.
I sometimes sprinkle bits of green pepper
or pimentos over rice for color.

52

Fish & Shellfish

53

SHRIMP NEWBURG
SERVES 4

1 pound cooked, peeled, and deveined shrimp
2 tablespoons butter
2 tablespoons flour
1 cup cream or half and half
3 tablespoons catsup
¾ tablespoon Worcestershire sauce
salt to taste
dash of Tabasco
⅛ teaspoon paprika
2 tablespoons cream sherry

Melt butter in sauce pan, stir in flour,
slowly add cream or half and half.
When sauce is smooth and thick, stir in
ketchup and Worcestershire sauce.
Stir in shrimp and seasonings, adjust to
taste if necessary. Immediately before serving, add sherry.
Serve over steamed rice.
Serves about 4 allowing 6-7 shrimp per person

Steamed Rice
1 cup long grained rice
2½ cup water
½ stick butter
1 teaspoon salt

Bring all to a boil, then reduce heat to very low and
continue to steam until done. Add additional water
if necessary. I often dot rice dish with tiny bits of
pimento peppers or green peppers where appropriate.

54

PARTY SALMON
SERVES 20-25

1 whole (boned) side of salmon
liquid smoke
garlic salt
lettuce leaves
fresh parsley
dill sauce (good mayonnaise & dill-weed to taste)

Line large baking pan with foil.
Wipe salmon dry on both sides.
Place salmon, skin side down in foil lined pan.
Rub salmon generously with liquid smoke, then garlic salt.
Turn fish skin side up and repeat process.
Lay a foil covering over fish and seal top and bottom together.
Place pan in 300 degree oven and bake about 45 minutes.
Check several times so as not to over bake.
Remove when done and chill several hours or overnight.
To serve, arrange lettuce leaves on large platter.
Place salmon on platter, skin side up. Remove skin if desired.
Garnish with lemon slices and fresh parsley.
The salmon may be scored in bite size pieces if desired.
Place bowl of dill sauce and tray of firm
crackers or Melba toast on side.
One side of salmon will serve about 25 for hors d'oeuvres,
depending on the size of the salmon.

55

BARBEQUE SALMON STEAKS
SERVES 6

6 salmon steaks approximately 1 ½ inch thick
soy sauce

Place salmon steaks in shallow pan.
Generously pour soy sauce over them.
Let the steaks marinate in the soy sauce
for a couple of hours.
Turn the steaks several times so as to
season both sides.
Cook on grill 4 minutes on one side
and 7 minutes on the other side.
Do not over cook.

A wood burning grill is best to use.

56

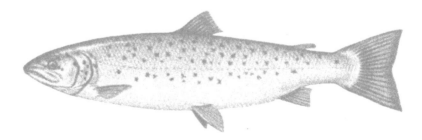

Scalloped Oysters
SERVES 4-6

1 pint oysters
½ cup melted butter
3 cups dry bread crumbs
½ cup cracker crumbs
½ teaspoon salt
¼ teaspoon pepper
½ tsp Worcestershire sauce
⅓ cup cream or half and half
⅓ cup oyster liquor

57

Drain oysters, set aside liquor, and check for shells.
Combine bread crumbs, cracker crumbs, butter, salt and pepper
Grease 1½ to 2-quart baking dish.
Cover the bottom of dish with a layer of the crumb mixture,
½ of the oysters, then another layer of crumbs,
then the rest of the oysters. Mix the cream or half and
half and oyster liquor together with the Worcestershire sauce.
Pour over oyster layer. Top with remaining crumbs, and
if you like, dot with a little butter. Bake in 400 degree
oven for about 20 minutes or until oyster edges curl.
Check to be sure crumbs are not scorching.

Salmon Cakes
SERVES 6

1 (16-oz.) can salmon
½ cup fine cracker crumbs
2 beaten eggs
½ teaspoon salt
butter or margarine
⅛ teaspoon paprika

Remove bone from salmon if desired.
Flake the salmon.
Add cracker crumbs, beaten eggs, salt and paprika.
Form into small round cakes.
Sauté in butter or margarine until lightly
browned on each side.

Quick and easy luncheon or early supper dish.
Could be served with dilled green beans and tiny
boiled potatoes and butter.

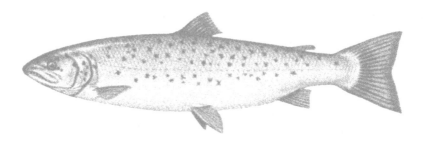

CRAB IMPERIAL
SERVES 6

¼ cup butter or margarine
¼ cup flour
2 cups milk
¼ teaspoon salt
¼ teaspoon pepper
dash Tabasco
1 egg yolk
2 tablespoons cream sherry
1 cup soft bread crumbs
2 teaspoons finely minced onion
2 teaspoons finely minced green pepper
¾ cup good mayonnaise
1 lb. back fin crab meat
⅔ cup buttered bread crumbs
⅛ teaspoon paprika

Melt butter or margarine, sauté onions and
green peppers, add slowly flour, milk, salt,
pepper and egg yolk, continue to stir over
low heat until all is blended well. Add paprika,
¼ cup mayonnaise, and soft bread crumbs.
Mix well and check seasoning. Adjust if necessary.
Remove from heat and add sherry.
Fold in crab meat carefully.
Spoon into a well buttered 1½ to 2-quart casserole,
glaze with remaining mayonnaise.
Top with buttered bread crumbs.
Sprinkle lightly with paprika.
Bake at 375 degrees for about 30 minutes.

SHRIMP AND CRAB DELUXE
SERVES 15

1 lb. regular crab meat
1½ lbs. shrimp cleaned and deveined
2½ cups cooked rice
2 cups finely cut celery
1/2 cup finely minced onion
2 (10 oz.)cans cream of mushroom soup
1 (8 oz.) can of water chestnuts cut in small pieces
1½ teaspoons Old Bay seasoning
½ cup dry sherry
1 tablespoon lemon juice
salt and pepper to taste
buttered bread crumbs

Pick over crab meat to remove any shell or cartilage.
Add cleaned and deveined shrimp.
Add cooked rice, celery, onion, Old Bay seasoning,
water chestnuts, cream of mushroom soup,
sherry, salt and pepper if necessary.
Mix all together well, if mixture seems too thick
you may add a little milk or other liquid.
Fill a 3-quart casserole and top with buttered crumbs.
Bake at 350 degrees for about 45 minutes,
until bubbly in the middle and crumbs
are lightly browned.

60

CRAB FLORENTINE
SERVES 8

2 tablespoons butter
2 (10-oz.) packages frozen chopped spinach
1 (10-oz.) can mushroom soup
1¼ cups prepared white sauce
1¼ cups shredded Swiss cheese
1 tablespoon fresh lemon juice
1 pound fresh crab meat
1 (6-oz.) can water chestnuts sliced
3 tablespoons grated Parmesan cheese

Melt butter in skillet, add drained spinach and cook
and stir until liquid has been absorbed.
Remove from heat and set aside.
Combine white sauce, lemon juice and shredded cheese
in sauce pan and cook over medium heat until cheese has melted.
Add crab meat, which has been picked over for cartilage,
add mushroom soup.
Butter a round 1½-quart casserole.
Put in ½ the spinach, then a layer,
using ½ the crab meat mixture,
repeat using the other half of the spinach
and top with the remaining half of the
crab meat and mushroom soup mixture.
Spread evenly and top with grated Parmesan cheese.
Bake 300 degrees about one hour.

*It may be prepared ahead and stored in a refrigerator.
In that case an additional 10 minutes, or so, should be
added to the baking time.

Meat & Poultry

63

CHICKEN MADELINE
SERVES 8

8 boneless, skinless, half chicken breasts
10-oz. bag unseasoned stuffing bread
2 cups chopped celery
4-5 tablespoons minced onion
3 extra large eggs
1 stick butter or margarine melted
poultry seasoning or celery salt to taste
¼ cup snipped parsley
chicken broth or warm water
1½ tablespoons tarragon flakes
½ cup sliced almonds
buttered crushed corn flakes

64

Mix together stuffing bread, celery, onion, eggs,
butter, seasonings, snipped parsley.
Add chicken broth or warm water enough to moisten.
Mix well, divide stuffing into 8 portions.
Flatten chicken breast on cutting board.
Place 1 portion of stuffing on wide end of breast
and roll up as you would a jelly roll.
Place in buttered and lightly salted 9 x 13 inch casserole.
Repeat with other seven portions.
Add about 1 cup water to casserole.
Brush breast with some melted butter, sprinkle lightly
with salt. Cover generously with corn flakes,
sprinkle with tarragon leaves and scatter
sliced almonds over all the chicken breasts. Cover with foil.
Bake 325 to 350 degree oven about 1¼ hours.
Test with sharp paring knife to be sure the breasts are done.
Remove foil the last 10 minutes of baking.
Serve hot with a dish of light chicken gravy or sauce.
Buttered green peas or other green vegetables
or a salad go nicely with this dish.

STUFFED PORK CHOPS
SERVES 6

6 thick, boneless pork chops
8-oz. package unseasoned stuffing bread
1 ½ cups chopped celery
½ cup minced fresh onion
½ cup butter or margarine (melted)
2 eggs
1 tablespoon. parsley flakes
milk, water, or chicken broth to moisten dressing
½ teaspoon celery salt
salt and pepper (if desired)

Order pork chops from market. They should be thick,
boneless and cut with a pocket.
Grease casserole and sprinkle lightly with salt.
Mix bread, celery, onion, eggs, celery salt and water,
milk, or chicken broth enough to moisten stuffing.
Add salt and pepper to taste.
Divide stuffing into 6 equal portions and stuff
each chop with a portion.
Place stuffed chops in casserole and add about
¾ cup water to casserole. Bake about 1 ½ hours
in a 350 degree oven.

Any stuffing left over may be baked in small container.
Sauer-Kraut is good to serve with the chops,
also baked apples.

65

BREADED VEAL CUTLETS
SERVES 4

4 veal cutlets
bread or fine cracker crumbs
salt, pepper, garlic powder or garlic salt
1 beaten egg diluted with 2 tablespoons water
butter or bacon drippings

Pat cutlets dry with a paper towel.
Season the bread crumbs with salt, pepper
and garlic powder or garlic salt.
Beat egg and add water, (you may have to double this).
Coat the cutlets with seasoned bread crumbs,
then dip into egg and water, then again into the crumb mix.
Heat butter or drippings and fry the cutlets until
brown on each side. This should be done over a quick heat.
Reduce heat to very low and cover and let the cutlets just
simmer until they are tender, (about ½ hour).

66

COUNTRY CHICKEN KIEV
SERVES 4

4 boneless, skinless halves of chicken breast
⅔ cup butter or margarine
½ cup bread crumbs
2 teaspoons grated Parmesan cheese
1 teaspoon dry basil leaves
1 teaspoon oregano leaves
½ teaspoon garlic salt
¼ teaspoon salt
¼ cup dry white wine
¼ cup finely cut green spring onions
¼ cup minced parsley

Preheat oven to 350-375 degrees

Melt butter or margarine in heavy sauce pan and set aside.
Combine Parmesan cheese, bread crumbs, basil,
oregano, garlic salt and salt and mix well.
Dip chicken first in butter then in bread crumb mixture.
Roll up chicken breast or if you prefer place flat in a baking dish.
Place in 350 degree heated oven and bake about 50 minutes or
until golden brown and tender.
Use remaining butter in which breast were
dipped to very lightly sauté green onions
and parsley, add wine.
When chicken is tender remove from oven,
pour wine sauce over and around chicken.
Return to oven 3-5 minutes to make sauce good and hot.
Sprinkle with a little fresh minced parsley and serve.

This recipe may be used for regular bone-in, skin-on
frying breast pieces. You may want to adjust measurements
of other ingredients if the pieces are larger.
Also adjust baking time.

ROAST TURKEY
SERVES 14-16

16-18 lb. plump turkey
3 (7-oz.) packages unseasoned stuffing bread
3 cups finely chopped celery
1 cup minced onion
5 eggs
1 stick melted butter
1 tablespoon parsley flakes
½ teaspoon poultry seasoning or celery salt
salt and pepper to taste
chicken bullion or warm milk to moisten stuffing

Wash and pat turkey dry. Salt body cavity and
also cavity at the neck. Mix all
stuffing ingredients together well.
Fill body cavity lightly and also the neck cavity with stuffing.
Draw loose skin at neck back over stuffing area
and tuck skin under turkey.
Tuck legs under band of skin at the tail.
Cover wings and neck and tail area lightly with foil.
Rub turkey with melted shortening (unsalted).
Add a couple cups of water to roasting pan.
Roast at 300 degrees about 20 minutes per pound.
Roast uncovered and baste frequently with pan drippings or water.
Season bird with salt, half way through roasting time.
If bird seems to be getting too brown, lay a piece of
foil lightly over top.
The stuffing mix may be varied by adding oysters, sausage,
mushrooms, apples, or raisins to dressing and seasoned to
suit your family. Any left over dressing may be baked in a small
casserole, perhaps adding a little more liquid to the dressing.

Beef Burgundy
SERVES 6-8

2½ pounds of one inch thick beef steaks
½ stick of margarine
½ cup chopped onion
½ cup flour
salt, pepper, garlic salt
fresh or small jar sliced mushrooms
about ¾ cup Burgundy wine
bits of parsley

Cut beef into one half inch cubes. Dredge with
flour, sprinkle lightly with salt, pepper, and garlic salt.
Brown beef in margarine, stirring often to brown evenly.
Sauté onions and mushrooms in about
one half stick of margarine and a tablespoon or so
of flour to make a light paste,
add enough water to make a sauce.
Mix well together, the beef and the onion mixture.
Place in a 275 or 300 degree oven (covered)
simmer about one and one half hours or
until beef is done. Adjust seasonings to taste,
adding water if necessary. Stir often to prevent sticking.
Add wine just before serving. Serve over cooked rice.
Parsley may be sprinkled over the cooked rice if desired.

69

BEEF STROGANOFF
SERVES 6-8

3 pounds round steak (cubed)
¾ cup flour
1 stick butter or margarine
1 (7-8 ounce) jar sliced mushrooms
or about 2 cups sliced fresh mushrooms
1 small onion minced
1 cup sour cream
salt and pepper
1-2 tablespoon Worcestershire sauce (if desired)
2 cubes bouillon

Season beef cubes with salt and pepper
and dust with flour. Sauté in butter or
margarine until lightly browned.
Remove from pan and lightly sauté onions
and mushrooms, add bouillon cubes
dissolved in one cup of water.
Stir beef and onions, etc. together well.
Place in heavy pan and simmer
about one hour or until beef is tender.
Add Worcestershire sauce if desired.
When ready to serve, stir in sour cream and mix well.
Serve over cooked noodles or cooked rice.

70

COUNTRY CURED HAM
SERVES ABOUT 35-40

1 whole country ham 14-15 lbs
½ lb. light brown sugar
pineapple preserves
2 sliced pineapple rings
couple maraschino cherries
whole cloves

Purchase whole country ham, preferably from a local
country butcher. It should be plump and aged 6 months
to 1 year. Scrub thoroughly with a brush to remove
salt and pepper. Soak in water a couple hours
or over-night: depending on the age of the ham.
Place in a large kettle and cover with water.
Cook slowly (simmering) about 5 or 6 hours
depending on the size of the ham, add extra water as needed.
When done remove from heat. Pour off broth.
When cooled, place ham on a rack in broiler pan
with ½ inch of water.
Remove rind and excess fat. Push whole cloves into the ham
in rows about ¾ inches apart.
Combine brown sugar, pineapple preserves or juice
enough to make a spreadable glaze. Garnish
with pineapple slices and cherries.
Place in 425 to 450 degree oven. Watch carefully,
add extra glaze and water as needed. Remove from
oven when ham is nicely glazed. To slice ham
thinly, cool over-night, slice and garnish
platter with fresh parsley.

The ham broth may be used to make bean soup,
cook green beans or kale, cabbage, etc., first remove
extra fat. The broth stores well in the refrigerator.

CORNED BEEF HASH PATTIES
MAKES 6 SERVINGS

1 pound can corned beef
2 cups (3 or 4) medium potatoes
1 small to medium onion
½ of one green pepper
1 stalk celery
½ teaspoon pepper
¾ cup light cream or half and half
4 tablespoons butter or margarine
buttered bread crumbs
snipped parsley

Cook potatoes in lightly salted water. Drain.
Put the cooked potatoes, corned beef, green pepper
and celery through the coarse blade of a food
grinder or a food processor.
Add black pepper.
Gradually add the light cream or half and half.
Form in patties, one inch thick and about 3 inches in diameter.
Pat on bread crumbs. Fry on both sides in the
melted butter or other fat.
Sprinkle on snipped parsley and serve

FAMILY MEAT LOAF
SERVES 6

2 cups soft bread crumbs or
¾ cup dried bread crumbs
2 eggs beaten
1 cup milk
1½ lbs. good ground beef
1/2 cup Hunt's tomato sauce, crushed canned tomatoes or ketchup
1½ tablespoons sugar
½ cup finely minced onion
⅓ cup finely minced green peppers
⅔ cup shredded cheddar cheese
1½ teaspoons garlic salt
¼ teaspoon pepper

Mix beaten eggs, milk, and bread crumbs.
Add sugar to the Hunt's sauce, tomatoes, or ketchup,
stir to blend, add garlic salt and pepper, cheese and ground beef.
Mix all together in a large bowl until beef, etc. are
blended, add a little more milk if necessary.
Mold into a nicely shaped loaf and bake in
a 350 degree oven for 45-60 minutes.
Cover lightly with a piece of foil to prevent loaf from drying out.
When done remove to a platter and garnish with fresh parsley.

The cheese and green peppers are optional.

CREAMED CHIPPED BEEF
SERVES 4

8 oz. package chipped beef
3 tablespoons butter
5 tablespoons minced onion or green onions
3 tablespoons flour
2 cups milk
minced parsley
2 tablespoons sherry (optional)

Separate chipped beef.
Sauté onions or green onions in
butter until lightly browned.
Sprinkle flour and pepper over the onions.
Slowly add milk and stir until smooth.
Add chipped beef and simmer until sauce thickens.
Remove from heat, add parsley and sherry.
Serve on hot buttered toast.

Salads & Dressings

HOT POTATO SALAD
SERVES 6-8

6 medium potatoes
8 slices bacon
½ cup fresh minced onion
1½ cups finely chopped celery
3 hard cooked eggs
⅓ cup vinegar
½ cup water
2 tablespoons sugar
2 beaten eggs
¼ teaspoon celery salt
minced parsley for a garnish

Cook potatoes in salted water. Cool and dice potatoes.
Dice hard cooked eggs and add to potatoes. Set aside.
Cut bacon into small pieces and sauté until crisp.
Remove from pan, save about one fourth of bacon for garnish,
Add the rest of the bacon to the potatoes and diced eggs.
Use about 3-4 tablespoons of bacon drippings to make dressing.
Sauté onions and celery in drippings until tender.
Then add beaten eggs, water, vinegar, sugar and celery salt.
Stir and cook until dressing bubbles through.
Pour over potatoes, etc. and mix very well.
Put all in a heavy pan and place in moderate oven (325 degrees)
Heat until hot through.
Garnish with parsley and reserved bacon.
Serve immediately.

76

STUFFED FRESH TOMATOES
SERVES 6

6 firm ripe tomatoes
3-4 cups chicken salad
lettuce leaves
sliced almonds
parsley sprigs

Place chilled tomatoes stems down. Cut each
tomato into six wedges. Spread wedges apart,
and sprinkle lightly with salt. Fill each tomato
with chicken salad. Serve on lettuce leaf.
Garnish with almonds or parsley sprigs.
The tomatoes may be used with shrimp or crab salad,
garnish with parsley sprigs, also pasta salad,
garnished with green pepper slices or parsley,
or potato salad garnished with hard-boiled egg slices.

77

PICKLED BEETS
SERVES 5-6

1 (#2) can tiny whole beets or sliced beats
½ cup vinegar
½ cup beet juice
½ cup sugar
½ teaspoon salt
2 tablespoons pickling spices

Drain beets well and set aside.
Add vinegar, sugar, salt, to juice.
Place spices in a cloth bag and add all to beet liquid.
Bring all to boil and simmer a few minutes.
Remove from heat and remove spice bag.
Pour liquid over beets and cover, let cool
and cover tightly. Serve very cold.

The spiced juice may be used to pickle hard
boiled eggs that can be used for a salad.

78

HAM SALAD
SERVES 6

2 cups ground or minced ham
1 cup finely chopped celery
½ cup sweet pickle, minced or ground
4 hard-cooked eggs (chopped)
sprigs of parsley
mayonnaise or sour cream dressing

Blend all ingredients together.
Serve with tomato wedges or
on lettuce leaf.
May also be used to make a hearty sandwich.

79

Molded Vegetable Salad
SERVES 12

3 packages lime Jell-O
4 cups water (very hot)
4½ cups finely diced vegetables
(equal parts cucumbers, carrots,
celery, unpeeled radishes and green peppers)
4 teaspoons very fine minced onion
1¼ teaspoons salt
lettuce leaves

Dissolve Jell-O in 4 cups hot water.
Cut vegetables very fine, add onion and salt.
Mix all together well.
When gelatin is about ready to set, fold in the vegetables.
Turn into a well oiled mold.
Chill until set or over night.
Unmold onto lettuce leaves.
Serve a good mayonnaise on the side.
I sometimes add finely shredded cabbage to
the vegetable mix. Lemon Jell-O may be used
instead of the lime Jell-O.

CRANBERRY SALAD MOLD
SERVES 12

16 oz. fresh cranberries
1 (20-oz.) can crushed pineapple
1 cup finely minced celery
1 orange (rind on)
1 cup sugar
2 packages lemon Jell-O
1 cup chopped pecans
1 cup boiling water

Cut orange(rind on) into sections and remove
seeds, if any. Grind or run orange and cranberries
through food processor. Add and mix the cup of sugar
with the cranberry, orange mix. Set aside.
Dissolve Jell-O in boiling water. When cooled,
mix celery and nuts together with the
cranberry and orange. Stir in and mix well
with the Jell-O which has been dissolved.
Pour into mold and refrigerate until firm.
Unmold on lettuce lined platter or plate.

81

Cole Slaw
Serves 8-10 Generously

1 medium head firm cabbage
2 crisp carrots
1½ cups mayonnaise
1 cup sugar
¼ cup vinegar
dash or two celery salt

Shred cabbage very, very fine,
shred carrots very, very fine,
I use my blender.
Drain both cabbage and carrots well.
Mix mayonnaise, vinegar, sugar and celery salt.
Beat until mixture is slightly glossy.
Adjust vinegar, sugar, etc. to suit your taste.
Mix cabbage and dressing.
Chill thoroughly before serving.

82

SPINACH SALAD
SERVES 6

1 pound fresh tender spinach
3 or 4 hard boiled eggs, sliced
½ pound bacon sautéed until crisp and crumbled
8 to 10 small mushrooms, sliced
⅔ cup salad oil
⅓ cup lemon juice or vinegar
⅓ cup of good mayonnaise
¼ teaspoon ground oregano (slight)
½ cup sugar
dash of garlic salt
dash of hot sauce

Clean and wash spinach through several waters,
drain well, break into bite size pieces.
Combine dressing ingredients in mixer
and mix well, adjust seasonings to taste.
Lightly toss spinach, eggs, bacon and mushrooms,
with just enough dressing to coat. Any left over
dressing may be refrigerated.
Serve at once.

83

CHICKEN SALAD
SERVES 10-12

9 cups cooked, cubed chicken
3 cups chopped celery
¾ cups minced sweet pickles
1 cup quartered green grapes
¾ cups sliced almonds
1½ cups good mayonnaise, more if needed

Mix the first five ingredients together.
Toss with mayonnaise.
Serve on lettuce leaf or in bowl,
garnish with fresh parsley.

84

BLACK CHERRY MOLD
SERVES ABOUT 15

3 packages black (bing) cherry Jell-O
1 (20-oz.) can crushed pineapple (drain and save juice)
1 (20-oz.) can black bing cherries (drain and save juice)
1 cup broken pecans
½ cup Angel Flake coconut
1 cup ginger ale
1 cup coca-cola
lettuce

Into a large bowl or pan pour the drained
pineapple and cherries.
Add nuts and coconut.
Add the coca-cola and ginger ale
which has been chilled.

Heat the pineapple juice and the cherry juice
and enough water to make 2 cups.
Dissolve the Jell-O in the hot juice.
When completely dissolved, remove from the heat
and add 2 cups of ice cold water and the
cola-cola and ginger ale mixture.
When mixture starts to jell pour into oiled mold.
Chill until firm.
Unmold onto lettuce covered plate.

LIME PARTY MOLD
SERVES 12

2 packages lime Jell-O
1 cup milk
16-20 marshmallows
1 20-oz. can crushed pineapple (undrained)
⅔ cup good mayonnaise
1 cup whipping cream
1 6-oz. cream cheese (room temperature)

Melt marshmallows in milk over very low
heat so as not to scorch them.
When marshmallows are all melted add Jello-O,
stir until dissolved, add cream cheese and stir all
ingredients until dissolved. Let mixture cool a bit.
When cool enough add mayonnaise to mixture.
Whip cream and fold into mixture. Mix well and
pour into oiled mold. Chill until set or over night.
Unmold onto lettuce covered serving platter.
Garnish with mandarin oranges, strawberries or grapes.

ORANGE MOLD

Follow same recipe, only use orange Jell-O
and garnish with sliced kiwi or green grapes.

STRAWBERRY MOLD

Follow same recipe, only strawberry Jell-O.
Garnish with green grapes, kiwi or strawberries with leaves on.

POTATO SALAD
SERVES 10-12

9 cups cooked and cubed potatoes
3 cups finely minced celery
⅔ cup minced onion (fresh)
6 hard cooked eggs
1⅔ cups good mayonnaise
⅓ cup vinegar
⅔ cup sugar
½ tablespoon prepared mustard
⅙ teaspoon celery salt

Cook potatoes in salted water, when done, cool and
cut them into small cubes. Chop the hard cooked eggs.
Toss together the potatoes, celery, onions, and chopped eggs.
In mixer, blend together mayonnaise, vinegar, sugar,
mustard and celery salt. Mix well. Taste the dressing.
Add a tiny bit more vinegar if you like a bit more tart flavor.
Pour dressing over potato mixture and mix well.
Refrigerate until ready to serve.

87

WALDORF SALAD DIVINE
MAKES ABOUT 6-8 SERVINGS

3 cups red, tart apples, unpeeled and diced
1 cup English walnuts, broken
1 cup chopped celery
1 cup drained mandarin oranges
6-8 snipped marshmallows
1 cup golden raisins (or regular)
¾ teaspoon lemon juice
3½ tablespoons good mayonnaise
2 tablespoons sugar
1 cup whipping cream

Toss together first 8 ingredients.
Whip cream until it will stand in peaks
adding sugar gradually. Fold gently
into fruit mixture. Chill well.

88

CUCUMBER MOUSSE
SERVE ABOUT 10-12

3 packages lime Jell-O
1 cup boiling water
3 firm cucumbers (nice size)
1 small onion
1 cup pecans chopped
1 cup mayonnaise
2 cups small curd cottage cheese
2 tablespoons vinegar

Dissolve Jell-O in boiling water. Grind cucumber and onion.
Mix well with mayonnaise, cottage cheese, and vinegar.
Add pecans. Mix all together thoroughly and pour
into mold and chill well or over night.
Unmold on platter and garnish with cucumber slices,
cherry tomatoes or water cress.

89

SEVEN LAYERED SALAD
SERVES ABOUT 20

2 firm heads iceberg lettuce
1 ½ cups frozen peas
1 ¼ cups finely chopped green peppers
1 ¼ cups minced onion
2 cups crumbled bacon or 1 cup bacon bits
2 cups shredded sharp cheddar cheese
½ cup granulated sugar
mayonnaise

Prepare bacon ahead so it is crisp and crumbled,
or if you prefer, use the bacon bits.
Rinse and drain heads of lettuce, let drain a bit.
Shred lettuce into a separate pan.
Using ⅓ of the lettuce, put in bottom of a large
punch bowl or suitable pan or bowl.
Using ⅓ of each ingredient, add to lettuce layer
following with, ⅓ each of the peas, peppers, onions,
bacon bits, sugar and shredded cheese in that order.
Glaze with mayonnaise to cover first layer.
Follow same procedure with a second layer,
cover with mayonnaise and then the third layer.
Spread mayonnaise carefully using only enough to cover nicely.
Cover bowl with Saran wrap first and then foil.
Refrigerate at least several hours.
When ready to serve, remove coverings and
toss salad lightly.
Serve on salad plates or guest may serve themselves.

The salad may be made in smaller quantities using the
same ingredients and procedure making just one or two layers.

SPECIAL SHRIMP SALAD
SERVES ABOUT 8-10

2½ pounds cooked, peeled, deveined shrimp
3 cups finely chopped celery
8 oz. small shell macaroni
1 cup salad oil
2 tablespoons vinegar or lemon juice
1 tablespoon dry sherry
¼ teaspoon hot sauce
1 cup good mayonnaise
1 tablespoon ketchup
½ teaspoon garlic salt
2 tablespoons sugar

If shrimp are large, I cut them into two or three pieces.
Cook macaroni shells according to package directions.
Mix together shrimp, celery and shells.
In mixing bowl blend together the oil, vinegar,
or lemon juice, sherry, hot sauce, mayonnaise,
ketchup, garlic salt and sugar.
Adjust dressing to suit your taste.
Mix shrimp with the dressing.
Chill well. Serve on lettuce leaf.

91

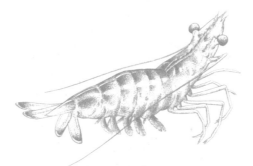

TOMATO ASPIC
SERVES ABOUT 8 PEOPLE

2½ cups tomato juice
2 envelopes unflavored Knox gelatin
½ cup cold water
¼ cup lemon juice
1 tablespoon Worcestershire sauce
2 tablespoons horse radish
2 tablespoons finely minced onion
½ cup tomato ketchup
¼ cup sugar (or to taste)
dash of Tabasco sauce
½ teaspoon salt or to taste
⅔ cup sliced stuffed olives (optional)

Dissolve gelatin in cold water.
Add dissolved gelatin to hot tomato juice, not boiling.
Stir until all gelatin has been dissolved.
Add rest of ingredients and mix thoroughly.
When aspic is about set, add olives if desired.
Pour in mold and chill thoroughly, or overnight.

FRESH TOMATOES AND MARINADE
SERVES 10-12

6 firm ripe red tomatoes
2 cups granulated sugar
½ cup vinegar
½ teaspoon dried basil leaves
½ teaspoon dried thyme leaves
¼ teaspoon celery salt
2 teaspoons onion flakes
garlic salt to taste
fresh parsley to garnish

Wash and slice tomatoes into ⅓ inch slices.
Arrange on serving dish.
Mix sugar, vinegar, basil, thyme, celery salt,
onion flakes and garlic salt, mix until
sugar, etc. are well blended.
Adjust or add any ingredient to taste.
Spoon marinade over tomatoes just before serving.
Garnish with fresh parsley.
Left over marinade will keep well in refrigerator.

93

DEVILED EGGS
SERVES 12

12 hard-boiled eggs
⅓ cup mayonnaise
2 tablespoons pickle juice or vinegar
¼ tablespoon prepared mustard
1½ tablespoons sugar
¼ teaspoon celery salt
tiny sprigs fresh parsley or dash paprika

I use medium eggs. Bring eggs to a boil
in salted water. When boiling, cut heat and
let them simmer about 20 minutes. Plunge eggs
into very cold or ice water. Peel and cut eggs
lengthwise. Remove the yolks. Place yolks,
mayonnaise, pickle juice or vinegar, mustard,
sugar and celery salt in mixer, and mix until it
becomes well blended. Adjust seasonings to your taste.
Run mixture through a ricer or sieve.
With a pastry bag fill egg whites.
Or use a spoon to fill the egg whites.
Garnish with sprigs of parsley or paprika.

94

SHRIMP PARTY MOLD
SERVES ABOUT 6

1 ½ tablespoons Knox gelatin
¼ cup water
1 small can tomato soup
9 oz. cream cheese softened
1 cup mayonnaise
¾ cup finely chopped celery
½ cup minced green onion
1 cup small shrimp or large shrimp cut in small pieces.
salt and pepper to taste
dash of Tabasco

Soak gelatin in cold water.
Heat tomato soup to boiling point.
Add softened gelatin and stir until mixture thickens.
Remove from heat and add remaining ingredients.
Pour into well oiled mold. Chill.
Unmold on lettuce leaves.

Cucumber and Onion Salad
YIELDS ABOUT 6 SERVINGS

3-4 firm cucumbers
2 medium size white onions
1¼ cups sour cream
2½ tablespoons vinegar
1 teaspoon salt
½ teaspoon pepper
dash celery salt if desired

Wash cucumbers and score rind with tines of fork. Slice.
Slice onions fairly thin.
Beat together well the sour cream, vinegar,
salt and pepper. Adjust seasonings if necessary.
Pour sour cream over onions and cucumbers.
Store in a covered container until ready to serve.

QUICK APPLE SALAD
SERVES 8

2½ cups diced apples
2½ cups diced celery
1¼ cups broken English walnuts or pecans
mayonnaise to moisten
lettuce

Wash, core, and dice apples.
Dice celery, and cut or break English walnuts or pecans.
Moisten well with mayonnaise.
Serve on lettuce leaf.
Quick and delicious.

97

CUCUMBER BOATS
SERVES 4

2 nice firm, well-shaped cucumbers
2½ cups of any tasty salad you may prefer
well seasoned salads
chicken salad
ham salad
shrimp salad
crab salad
shredded lettuce or watercress

Wash cucumbers well, cut in halves
length-wise and scoop out seeds.
Fill with any of the above salads and
serve on a bed of shredded lettuce or watercress.

This makes a quick, hearty, luncheon dish.

98

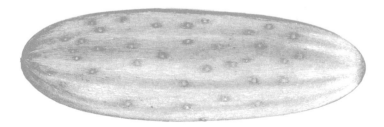

PASTA SALAD
SERVES 8-10

1 (8-oz.) package Rotini Pasta
½ pound mild ham (cut into small cubes)
½ pound shredded sharp cheese
1 cup minced onion
2 cups diced celery
1 cup ripe olives (sliced)

DRESSING
1 cup salad or olive oil
½ cup vinegar
1 teaspoon oregano leaves
½ cup tomato ketchup
½ cup sugar
½ cup mayonnaise
2-3 dashes Tabasco
garlic salt to taste

Cook pasta according to package directions.
Rinse and drain well.
Mix together dressing ingredients.
Toss together pasta, ham, cheese, celery,
onions and sliced olives.
Fold in dressing and mix well.
Cover and refrigerate.

Vegetable Dishes

STEAMED BROCCOLI AND CAULIFLOWER

SERVES 6-8

1 small head cauliflower
2 small broccoli heads
salt and pepper
butter melted
pimento pepper bits
shredded sharp cheddar cheese or cheese sauce (optional)

Wash thoroughly broccoli and cauliflower and
cut into small flowerets.
In lightly buttered baking dish, alternate broccoli
and cauliflower, stems down in horizontal rows.
Add about ½ cup water to dish.
Sprinkle lightly with salt and pepper. Cover tightly.
Steam in 325-350 degree oven for about
15-20 minutes or until tender.
Cheese or cheese sauce may be added, if desired,
remove cover, allow perhaps 5 minutes, in oven,
more for the cheese to melt.
Using a metal pan, broccoli and cauliflower may
be covered and steamed on very low heat
on stove top. When tender, drizzle with melted butter
and garnish with pimento bits.

102

Lemony Brussels Sprouts
SERVES 4-6

2 (10-oz.) packages of fresh Brussels sprouts
⅓ cup melted butter or margarine
1 tablespoon fresh lemon juice
salt and pepper to taste

Cook Brussels sprouts in lightly salted water until tender.
Melt butter or margarine and combine it with the lemon juice.
Pour butter and lemon juice over sprouts and serve.

103

SAUTÉED EGGPLANT
SERVES 4

1 nice firm eggplant
flour
salt
bit of paprika
butter or cooking oil

Peel and slice eggplant into ¼ inch slices.
Mix flour, salt and paprika.
Dredge eggplant slices in flour mixture,
and fry in butter until lightly browned.
They may be dipped in egg and then
buttered bread crumbs or cornmeal and then deep fried.
In that case add 2 tablespoons water to one egg, beat,
then bread crumbs or cornmeal.
Then deep fry until lightly browned.

The above procedure may also be used for summer squash.

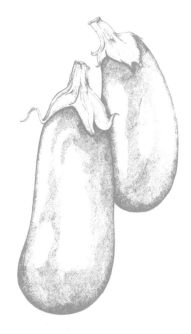

FRIED ZUCCHINI
SERVES 4-5

1 or 2 firm zucchini
1 or 2 beaten eggs
salt and pepper
lightly buttered bread crumbs
butter or cooking oil

Wash and dry zucchini.
Cut into round slices or lengthwise slices.
Beat eggs, salt and pepper together.
Put buttered crumbs in separate bowl.
Dip each slice first in crumbs, then in beaten eggs,
and again in buttered crumbs.
Let stand a few minutes, then deep fry
in cooking oil or sauté in butter or oil in frying pan.

105

PARSLEYED NEW POTATOES
SERVES 4-5

8-10 small new potatoes
lightly salted water to cover
2 tablespoons butter
2 tablespoons flour
1 cup milk
salt and pepper to taste
fresh minced parsley (tablespoon or two)

Cook potatoes in their jackets in the salted water.
Drain and peel them when they are cooked tender.
Make a sauce with the butter, flour and milk.
Melt the butter, stir in the flour keep on
low heat so as not to brown the flour.
Gradually add the milk and salt and pepper.
Cook until smooth and thickened.
Add a little extra milk if the sauce seems too thick.
Pour over the hot potatoes and sprinkle with
minced parsley.

GREEN PEAS AND ONIONS
SERVES 6-8

2 (10-oz. packages) frozen peas
1 (10-oz. package) tiny pearled onions
1 tablespoon sugar
½ cup butter or margarine
salt and pepper to taste
light white sauce to thicken if desired

Cook peas and onions in a minimum amount of water.
Add butter, salt, pepper, and sugar.
When tender the white sauce may be added if desired.
Or when the peas and onions are tender,
they may be drained of the remaining liquid and
then, pour the melted butter over them just before serving.

Also sliced or tiny mushrooms may be used
instead of the onions.

107

SPINACH SOUFFLÉ
SERVES 6-8

10-oz. package of frozen chopped spinach
8-oz. sharp cheddar cheese shredded
1 lb. cottage cheese (small curd)
3 eggs beaten
3 tablespoons flour (rounded)
1 teaspoon salt

Beat eggs, salt, flour together in mixer. Add
to thawed spinach, shredded cheese and cottage cheese.
Mix all together well. Spoon into casserole and bake
uncovered in 325 degree oven for about
40-45 minutes or until set.
Double for 3 quart casserole.

If recipe is doubled you may add an extra
5-6 oz of spinach to the recipe.
I sometimes do.

BAKED STUFFED GREEN PEPPERS
SERVES 4

4 green pepper cases
2 tablespoons butter or bacon drippings
3 tablespoons minced onions
½ pound good ground beef
½ teaspoon salt
1 cup cooked rice
buttered bread crumbs
shredded cheddar cheese

Cut off tops of peppers, wash and remove seeds.
Sauté beef in butter or drippings.
Add onions and sauté lightly.
Mix together rice and meat, add salt
or a little seasoning salt or ¼ teaspoon Worcestershire sauce.
Stuff peppers with mixture.
Top with bread crumbs and shredded cheese.
Place in shallow pan. Add about ½ inch of
water or enough to keep peppers from scorching.
Bake in 350 degree oven about 20 minutes or
until peppers are tender.

Peppers may be stuffed with a macaroni cheese mix,
cheese, rice, and tomatoes or any compatible
vegetable mixture or cold, uncooked, with slaw,
potato salad or ham salad.
A combination of ground beef, fresh corn, tomato, cheese and
buttered bread crumbs is also very good
when served baked and hot.

FRESH COOKED KALE
SERVES ABOUT 6

3-4 pounds fresh kale
½ pound bacon sautéed until crisp and minced
salt

Wash kale thoroughly in several changes of fresh water.
Remove any coarse stems. Place in pot with a small
amount of water, sprinkle very lightly with salt.
Cover and cook slowly, about twenty five minutes until tender.
It will have cooked down dramatically.
Add the minced bacon, a little butter or a tablespoon
or two of the bacon drippings and
cook two or three minutes more.
Have a small cruet of vinegar on the table as some folks like to
sprinkle a little vinegar over the kale. Boiled, buttered,
potatoes, or macaroni are nice to serve with the kale.

110

ASPARAGUS SUBLIME
SERVES 6-8

2½ cups fresh asparagus cut in ½ inch pieces
½ pound shredded sharp cheddar cheese
1 pound cottage cheese
3 eggs
1 teaspoon salt
3 tablespoons flour
buttered bread crumbs

Cook asparagus in water about five minutes.
Drain, add cottage cheese, sharp cheese.
Beat together eggs, flour and salt and
mix thoroughly with asparagus, cheese,
and cottage cheese. Put into casserole.
Cover lightly with bread crumbs.
Bake in 300-325 degree oven until set
about 40 minutes.

111

Marinated Green Beans
SERVES 8-10

2 lbs. French cut green beans
2 or 3 sliced medium sized onions
½ cup good olive oil
2 teaspoons lemon juice
1 teaspoon pepper
2 teaspoons minced parsley
½ teaspoon sugar
salt to taste

Steam beans for a few minutes.
Drain, cool, add sliced onions.
Mix other ingredients together and blend well.
Pour marinade over vegetables, cover, store in refrigerator.
Cauliflower flowerets, marinated the same way might be
a good companion for the beans.

SUPER CAULIFLOWER
SERVES 4-6

1 medium head of cauliflower
1 cup sour cream
4 oz. sharp cheddar cheese shredded
light sprinkle of salt and pepper

Wash head of cauliflower and cut into flowerets.
Cook a few minutes in very lightly salted water, then drain.

Grease 1½ or 2-quart casserole dish.

Using one half of each ingredients place a layer
of cauliflower, then sour cream, then sharp cheese and
lightly sprinkle salt and pepper.
Repeat with remaining half of ingredients.
Bake in 350 degree oven 10-12 minutes,
or until cheese is well melted.

113

Mashed Potato Cakes
MAKES 4-5 SMALL CAKES

2 cups left-over mashed potatoes
½ stick butter or margarine
flour
dash of pepper (if desired)

Pat cold mashed potatoes into small round flat cakes.
Melt butter or margarine in frying pan.
Pat the cakes with flour and brown in the butter or margarine.
When brown on one side, turn them over carefully,
and brown on the other side, Serve immediately.

This is an excellent way to use left over mashed potatoes.
You can add a bit of fresh minced onion, onion flakes,
crumbled bacon, or left over bits of country sausage
which has already been cooked. Mix as before and fry
in the butter or margarine as before.

114

FRESH VEGETABLE TRAY AND DIP
YIELD 2 CUPS DIP

cauliflower
broccoli
carrots
cucumbers
celery
green peppers
radish roses
cherry tomatoes or other garnish

Wash and cut cauliflower and broccoli into small flowerets.
Wash, peel carrots and cut carrots and celery
into thin 3 inch strips.
Repeat with green pepper.
Wash and score, with a sharp fork, the unpeeled cucumber.
Slice in rounds.
Arrange vegetables on a large round plate or
sectioned relish tray.
A bowl for the dip can be put into the middle of the tray
or set beside the vegetable tray.
I like to arrange the cucumber slices in the outer edge of
the tray. Garnish with radish roses, cherry tomatoes
or other fresh vegetables.

Dip
1 cup good mayonnaise
1 ½ cups sour cream
1 tablespoon finely minced onion or chives
2 tablespoons lemon juice
1 clove crushed garlic or garlic salt to taste
anchovy paste to taste

In mixer combine all ingredients, chill until serving time.
Makes 2 cups.

115

STEAMED CABBAGE
SERVES 4-6

1 medium firm head of new cabbage
6-8 strips cured bacon
black pepper
½ cup water

Place bacon strips in 325 degree oven on middle rack
in broiler pan to crisp. Or cut bacon in ½ inch pieces
and sauté in skillet until it is crisp, stirring frequently
so it will cook evenly.
When crisp remove from pan and drain.

Wash and trim cabbage head, cut into 4 to 6 wedges
depending on size of the cabbage head.
Remove the firm core. Place cabbage wedges
in heavy deep pan. Pepper lightly.
Lay crisp bacon slices or small pieces over the cabbage.
Add ½ cup of water to pan before covering pan to cook
Cover pan tightly and let the cabbage get hot.
Then cut back the heat and steam the cabbage slowly,
about 20 minutes, depending on the size
of the cabbage wedges. Check often,
little or no salt is needed. Don't over cook.

Delicious! Good with plain quartered boiled
or baked buttered potatoes.

SAUER-KRAUT
SERVES ABOUT 12

2 (29-oz.) cans Sauer-Kraut
2½ lbs. boneless fresh pork spareribs
⅛ tsp of pepper (optional)

Cover kraut with tepid water and rinse well
and drain off water. Cut pork into about 2 inch pieces
and mix into the kraut. Place small amount of fresh water
in cooking pot, add kraut and pork
and cook on very low heat until pork pieces are done;

about 1½ hours, don't over cook.

If you use bone-in-spareribs
you have to have about twice as many pounds.

This is an excellent dish to serve with mashed potatoes
at Thanksgiving and Christmas dinner.

117

FRIED GREEN TOMATOES
SERVES 4

4 unpeeled green tomatoes
equal portions light brown sugar and flour
salt and pepper
butter
fresh snipped basil or dry basil leaves

Wash and slice tomatoes into ½ inch slices.
Mix together brown sugar and flour salt and pepper.
The basil may be mixed with the flour etc.
or be used as a garnish.
Pat the flour mixture on the tomatoes.
Sauté in butter, being careful not to let them
burn, until they are light brown and cooked through.

118

DOWN HOME GREEN BEANS
SERVES 6-8

2 pounds fresh green beans
ham broth or bits of sliced ham to season
½ cup minced fresh onion or ¼ cup onion flakes
salt and pepper to taste

Wash and string fresh string beans.
Break or cut into one or one and a half inch pieces.
Cook in ham broth or add bits of sliced ham
or crumbled bacon to water in which beans are cooked.
You can even season with bacon drippings,
a couple of tablespoons full. Use the fresh minced onion
or onion flakes in either case.

Years ago folks would sometimes drop in the pot
a few small, whole pared potatoes and cook them all together.
Saved time on their busy days. With a slice or two of ham,
the beans and potatoes, some home made applesauce,
fresh homemade bread and newly churned butter,
and piece of cherry pie, "dinner", at twelve noon,
would all be ready when the "men" came
in from the fields to eat.

119

HERBED GREEN BEANS
SERVES ABOUT 6

1 pound fresh green beans (cut)
¼ cup butter
½ cup chopped onion
½ clove minced garlic
¼ cup chopped celery
½ cup minced parsley
¼ teaspoon rosemary
¼ teaspoon basil
¾ teaspoon salt

Cook green beans and drain. Melt butter and sauté onion, garlic, and celery. Add parsley, rosemary, basil, and salt. Cover and simmer 10 minutes. Toss the herb flavored butter with the hot green beans and serve.

FRIED SWEET CORN
SERVES 6

4 cups corn from cooked roasting ears
½ cup butter or margarine
½ cup minced green peppers (optional)
½ teaspoon salt (less if corn has been salted)
sprinkle of pepper

Combine all ingredients and sauté in butter
about 15 to 20 minutes, stirring constantly
as it burns easily.

This is a wonderful way to use up
left-over roasting ears.

121

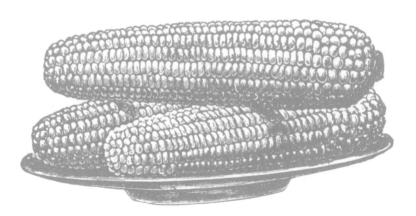

Left Over
Country Fried Potatoes
SERVES ABOUT 3-4

2-3 cups pan fried potatoes
2-3 eggs
⅓ cup onion flakes or fresh onion
dash of pepper
½ stick of butter or margarine

Melt butter in frying skillet, add potatoes
and allow them to get hot, add eggs and pepper
stirring and turning until eggs are cooked.
Serve immediately.

Crisp crumbled bacon or left over sausage can
be sliced or crumbled and added to the dish
to add flavor and nutrition.

122

YUMMY SWEET POTATOES
SERVES 8-10

6 cups cooked and mashed sweet potatoes
1 cup light brown sugar
3 tablespoons butter (melted)
1 teaspoon ground cinnamon
1 teaspoon vanilla
1 cup milk
1 cup broken pecans

Cook sweet potatoes in salted water or use
canned sweet potatoes.
Mash in mixer until all lumps have been blended in.
Add melted butter, brown sugar,
cinnamon, vanilla and milk.
Blend all together well.
Turn into a 2-quart casserole.
Bake in 375 degree oven about 35 minutes.
Top with pecans the last 5 minutes of baking.
If you prefer you can substitute small
marshmallows for topping
instead of the pecans.

123

SUMMER SQUASH IN SOUR CREAM
SERVES 4-5

2 lbs. young tender summer squash
2 tablespoons butter or bacon drippings
⅓ cup minced onion
1 cup sour cream
1 tablespoon flour
salt and pepper to taste
dash of paprika
parsley sprigs for garnish

Wash, peel and seed squash if necessary.
Cut into thick slices and quarter the slices.
Cook the squash covered in a very small amount
of lightly salted water.
There should be very little water left in the pan.
Drain squash. Hold in strainer.
Melt the butter in pan, stir in the onion, sauté onion
for a minute add flour and sour cream and
bring these ingredients to a boil.
Stir until smooth.
Combine squash and sour cream, flour mixture.
Put in serving dish and garnish with parsley.

SUMMER SUCCOTASH
SERVES ABOUT 8

1 cup chopped celery
½ cup minced onion
2 cups fresh or frozen baby lima beans
2 cups fresh or frozen whole kernel corn
4 tablespoons butter
1 tablespoon sugar
salt and pepper to taste
light white sauce to thicken if desired

Cook corn and baby lima beans in about 1½ to 2 cups
lightly salted water on low heat.
Lightly sauté onions and celery in butter
and add them to corn and lima beans.
Add celery, onion, butter, and sugar to simmering
corn and lima beans. Cook until tender.
Serve as is or add the light sauce to thicken slightly.
Season to taste.

The succotash may be made with canned vegetables,
but I much prefer the fresh vegetables.

125

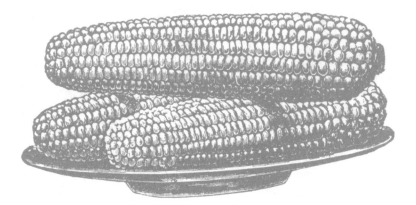

GLAZED BABY CARROTS
SERVES 4-6

4 cups canned baby carrots
1 cup light brown sugar
1 ½ teaspoons ground ginger
½ stick butter or margarine

Bring carrots to boil in about half their juice.
Add brown sugar, butter and ginger.
Let them boil about five minutes to flavor well,
or blend half the carrot juice, sugar, ginger,
and butter and bring to a boil and simmer
a few minutes to make a light syrup.
Pour hot syrup over hot drained carrots and serve.

If the carrots can remain in syrup
they will be better flavored.

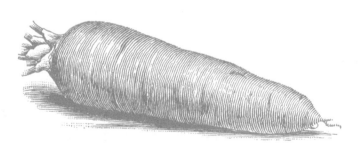

POTATOES AU GRATIN
YIELDS 6-8 SERVINGS

5-6 medium size potatoes
½ stick of butter
3 tablespoons flour
1 ½ cups milk
1 teaspoon salt
1 ½ cups shredded cheddar sharp or longhorn cheese
1 ½ tablespoons onion flakes
1 ½ cups cubed cheese
salt and pepper to taste

Peel and slice potatoes. Parboil in lightly salted water.
When potatoes are still firm remove from heat and drain.
Melt butter and make a sauce of flour, pepper and milk,
heating and stirring until smooth.
Prepare buttered casserole and alternate
layers of potatoes, cheese, onion flakes and sauce,
add extra milk to casserole if necessary.
Dot with cubed cheese.
Cover sparingly with buttered bread crumbs.
Bake in 325 degree oven for about 45 minutes or
until the potatoes are well done.

You can mix all the ingredients together gently,
top with cheese cubes and top with
bread crumbs and bake.

127

LEFT OVER MASHED POTATOES AND HAM CAKES

SERVES 4

1 cup mashed potatoes
1 cup ground cooked ham
1 tablespoon minced parsley
¼ teaspoon Worcestershire sauce
salt and pepper if necessary
a little onion juice or onion flakes (optional)
melted butter or margarine

Mix all together until well blended.
Pat into uniform flat cakes.
Pat on a dusting of flour.
Sauté on both sides until light brown.

Excellent way to use left-over mashed potatoes
and ham from a family dinner. Could be
the next day's lunch.

EASY BAKED BEANS
SERVES 6-8

1 (40½-oz.) can Great Northern beans
4 or 5 slices bacon
½ cup minced onion or 2 tablespoons dried onion flakes
⅔ cup light brown sugar
2 tablespoons dark molasses
1 tablespoon prepared mustard
3 tablespoon catsup

Cut bacon into ½ inch pieces and sauté until crisp.
Reserve small quantity of crisp bacon to garnish serving dish.
Mix often and bake until beans are soft and
liquid is thickened nicely and beans are well seasoned.
Garnish with reserved bacon.

If preferred, bacon may be cut in small pieces and
added to bean mixture and baked in with
all the rest of the ingredients.
If preferred, sliced hot dogs may be substituted
for the bacon.

129

GREEN BEAN DELUXE
SERVES 6-8

1 (16-oz.) package frozen French cut beans
1 (10-oz.) can mushroom soup
1 cup finely diced celery or
1 small can of celery soup.
onion flakes
1 cup crisp bacon pieces
crushed buttered corn flakes
fried onion rings or pieces
½ cup water
sliced almonds (optional)

Place green beans in 2-quart casserole,
salt and pepper lightly.
Sprinkle with a few onion flakes (if desired).
Cover with the diced celery or the celery soup.
Spread the crisp bacon over the casserole,
cover with the mushroom soup.
Top with either the corn flakes and almonds or
the fried onion rings or pieces.
Place casserole in 350 degree oven for 40-50 minutes
or until beans are tender.

Desserts

STEWED PRUNES
SERVES 4-6

1 pound dried pitted prunes
hot water to cover
½ to ¾ cup sugar
1 tablespoon lemon juice or
1 teaspoon cinnamon

Soak prunes in hot water about one hour.
Cook gently about 30 minutes.
Cool and serve.

They are excellent as a garnish for various meat plates.
They also may be spiced.
In that case cook them about 30 minutes.
Drain them and make the following syrup.

Spice Syrup
To the prune juice add
1 cup brown sugar
½ cup vinegar
2 tablespoons lemon juice
2 sticks cinnamon
⅓ teaspoon nutmeg
⅓ teaspoon allspice
⅓ teaspoon whole cloves

Bring syrup to a boil.
Add prunes and cook a minute or so.
Cool and place prunes in container and
pour over them the syrup.
Cover jar or container.
Store in refrigerator.

STEWED APPLES AND RAISINS
SERVES 6-8

12 large firm tart apples, not sauce apples
1 cup sugar
⅛ teaspoon salt
about 2 cups water
1½ cups seedless raisins
1 or 2 sticks cinnamon

Wash and pare 12 firm apples.
Core and slice apples.
Boil water, sugar and salt together about 3 minutes.
Add cinnamon sticks.
Add apples and raisins and cook gently
until they are done, just tender.
Do not over cook.

These are a nice healthful dish that
can be used as a mid-afternoon snack

133

RICE PUDDING
SERVES 4

2½ cup milk
½ cup long grain rice (uncooked)
½ cup sugar
½ cup seedless raisins
1 teaspoon vanilla
light cream and light brown sugar

Combine rice, milk, sugar, salt and raisins in a
heavy sauce pan. Bring to a boil.
Reduce heat to very low heat and cook covered
until rice is tender and milk is absorbed.
Stir often and keep covered except for the time you stir rice.
Add a bit more milk if necessary.
Add vanilla the last few minutes of cooking and stir well.
Serve with light cream and a sprinkle of
light brown sugar if desired.

134

99 LBS. NET WEIGHT

WHOLE BEAN
UNCOATED

TABLE RICE

DELECTABLE APPLE CRISP
SERVES 8-10

6 nice size firm apples
1½ cups light brown sugar
1 cup all purpose flour
¼ teaspoon salt
¾ cup chopped pecans
½ cup softened butter
½ teaspoon ground cinnamon

Toppings
whipped cream
vanilla ice cream
marshmallow sauce

Peel, core and dice apples and put into a
rectangular baking dish.
Cover with ½ the light brown sugar.
Combine the rest of the sugar and the salt, pecans,
cinnamon, flour and softened butter and blend
all together with a pastry blender or wire beater on mixer.
When completely mixed and crumbly, cover apples well,
the top, sides and edges making sure
all apples are completely covered.
Bake in 350 degree oven about 1 hour.
Serve warm and top with sweetened and
flavored whipped cream, a small scoop of vanilla ice cream
or a marshmallow sauce.

See marshmallow sauce in index.

135

ICE CREAM CAKE
YIELDS 8 OR 9 SERVINGS

1 recipe any flavor cake
yellow, white, chocolate, spice, etc.
1 (½ gal.) rectangular carton ice cream (2 x 6½ inch)
vanilla, chocolate, strawberry, etc.
frosting to cover

Mix and bake cake in a 15 x 10 inch jelly roll pan.
Cool and cut into equal 3½ inch wide, 7½ inch long slices.
Starting with cake, as bottom layer, alternate cake with
2 slices ice cream about ½ inch thick.
With knife, smooth sides and ends of loaf
and frost immediately, with frosting of your choice.
Decorate if desired.

It is important to have all ingredients ready to
use and the ice cream firm.
Place in freezer immediately, store there
until ready to serve.

Baked Bread Pudding
SERVES 6

2¼ cups milk
2 slightly beaten eggs
1 teaspoon vanilla
½ teaspoon ground cinnamon
¼ teaspoon salt
2 slices day old bread (cubed ¾ inch)
½ cup packed light brown sugar
½ cup seedless raisins.

Combine milk, eggs, vanilla, cinnamon and salt.
Fold in cubed bread, stir in brown sugar and raisins.
Mix well. Pour into 8 x 2 inch round casserole.
Set casserole in a baking pan.
Pour hot water in to a depth of 1 inch around the casserole.
Bake at 350 degrees about 45 minutes or until
a knife comes out clean.

137

YUMMY APPLESAUCE PUDDING
SERVES 6-8

8 slices day old white bread
2 cups applesauce
½ cup seedless raisins
¼ cup packed light brown sugar
½ teaspoon ground cinnamon
2½ cups milk
2 eggs
½ cup light brown sugar (packed)
½ teaspoon vanilla
¼ teaspoon salt

Topping
Mix together, 1 tablespoon brown sugar, 1 tablespoon
flour, 1 teaspoon ground cinnamon and ½ cup chopped pecans.

Butter an 8 x 8 x 2 inch baking dish.
Butter 4 slices of bread and
put in buttered casserole, buttered side up.
Mix applesauce, raisins, 2 tablespoons brown sugar and
½ teaspoon cinnamon, spoon this mixture
over buttered bread evenly.
Cut the remaining 4 slices of bread into triangles
and arrange over applesauce to cover well.
Beat together the 2½ cups milk, the 2 eggs and ½ cup
brown sugar, ½ teaspoon vanilla and ¼ teaspoon salt.
Pour over second layer of bread evenly.
Mix the topping and sprinkle over eggs etc.
Bake at 350 degrees for about 50-55 minutes.

A spoon of whipped cream or Cool Whip can only
make it better when you serve it.

138

TINY PECAN TARTS
YIELDS ABOUT 4 DOZEN TARTS

Shells
6 oz. cream cheese (softened)
1 cup butter or margarine
2 cups flour
¼ teaspoon salt

Mix together cream cheese, butter or margarine,
salt and flour to make a soft dough.
Roll the dough into tiny balls about ¾ to 1 inch in diameter.
Place dough balls into tea size muffin tins,
Shape into tiny tart shells. Set aside.

Filling
2 eggs
1 ½ cups brown sugar
2 tablespoons soft butter
2 teaspoons vanilla
⅔ cup chopped pecans
pinch of salt

Beat together butter and brown sugar until fluffy,
add eggs, vanilla, salt and pecans. Mix well.
If you prefer the pecans may be put in shells
first and then spoon in egg, sugar mixture into each shell.
Bake at 325 degree about 25 minutes. Bake them, cool slightly
and remove from tins.
The baked shells may also be used for tiny quiches and
pumpkin tarts, also cherry or blueberry pie filling or mincemeat.
In that case the shells should be baked first and then filled.

139

AMBROSIA DELIGHT
SERVES 8-10

1 ½ cups diced oranges or mandarin orange sections
1 cup green or red seedless grapes (quartered)
½ cup regular or golden seedless raisins (optional)
4 sliced bananas
½ cup angel flake or fresh grated coconut
5 snipped marshmallows
¾ cups broken pecans or macadamia nuts
3 teaspoons lemon juice
¾ cup whipping cream
2 teaspoons good mayonnaise
lettuce

Combine oranges, grapes, raisins, coconut,
marshmallows and nuts and lemon juice.
Whip cream, gradually add mayonnaise.
Stir into fruit, mix well, chill.
Serve on lettuce leaf, garnish with a
little extra coconut or nut pieces.

140

BUTTER CREAM MINTS
MAKES ABOUT 70 LITTLE MINTS

1 lb. 10x sugar
¼ pound butter (1 stick)
3 tablespoons warm water
10-14 drops peppermint oil or extract to taste
pink, green, or any coloring you may choose

Cream together sugar and butter until soft and fluffy.
Beat in warm water.
Add peppermint flavoring, slowly mix in 10x sugar,
scrape sides and bottom of bowl and blend all together well.
Press mint mixture into tiny rose, bell or other molds.
If you don't have molds, roll mixture into
½ inch round long rolls.
Cut into about 1 inch little pillow shaped mints.
When set well, put into tiny paper cups if desired.

LEMON FLUFF DESSERT
SERVES 6-8

1 (3oz) package lemon Jell-O
juice and rind of 1 nice firm lemon
½ cup sugar
1 (12 oz) can Pet evaporated milk (chilled)
Graham Cracker Crumb mix

Graham Cracker Mix
2½ cups Graham cracker crumbs
½ cup sugar
⅔ cup butter or margarine (room temperature)

Mix together the Graham cracker crumbs, sugar
and butter or margarine until well-blended.
Press 1/2 of this mixture into bottom of a 9 x 9″
or 9 x 13″ pan or casserole dish
(depending on the thickness of dessert desired).

Prepare Jell-O according to package directions.
Mix together lemon juice and grated lemon rind and sugar.
When Jell-O is slightly cooled blend it with lemon juice mixture.
In separate bowl, beat chilled Pet milk
until it is the consistency of whipped cream.

Fold whipped milk into lemon Jell-O mix.
Blend thoroughly and pour into crumb-lined pan or casserole dish.
Top with the second half of the crumb mix.
Chill several hours or over night. Cut into squares.
Top with a twist of lemon rind
or a dollop of whipped cream if desired.

FRUIT IN WATERMELON SHELL

1 watermelon
1 cantaloupe
1 honeydew
grapes
strawberries
blueberries
any fresh fruit
leaf lettuce

Draw a line with a paring knife around the top
fourth of the watermelon.
Try to make the lines meet when
you completely circled the melon.
Cut off the top fourth of the melon with a large sharp knife.
With a melon baller scoop out the meat of the melon.
Carve the top of the melon shell in a saw-tooth fashion
making cuts about ½ inch deep. Scrape and drain shell well.
Ball out the rest of the melons.
Place watermelon on large lettuce covered tray and fill
with fruit alternating the various kinds.
Garnish base of melon with grapes, nectarines or any
small fruits in season. Use extra fruit to refill melon.

* The filled melon makes a lovely addition to any
summer picnic table.

143

Cakes & Cookies

DAINTY LEMON DELIGHTS
MAKES ABOUT 4 DOZEN

3 egg whites
⅔ cup Crisco oil
2 teaspoons vanilla
1 teaspoon finely grated lemon rind
¾ cup granulated sugar
2 cups sifted all purpose flour
2 teaspoons baking powder
½ teaspoon salt

Sift together flour, baking powder and salt.
Beat egg whites lightly.
Gradually stir in oil and lemon rind and vanilla
continue beating adding the sugar gradually
until the mixture thickens
Add flour mixture a little at a time until all is well blended.
Drop the dough by teaspoonful onto ungreased cookie sheet.
Drop cookies about 2½ inch apart
allowing them space to spread.
Grease the bottom of a water glass with oil, dip the
bottom into granulated sugar and press dropped
cookies to flattened them.
Bake in 350 to 400 degree oven until very lightly browned.
Remove from cookie sheet as soon as they
are taken out of the oven.
Makes about 4 dozen 2½ inch cookies.

146

DATE TORTE
YIELDS ABOUT 24-26 PIECES

1 cup sugar
2 heaping tablespoons flour
1 teaspoon baking powder
a pinch of salt
3 well beaten egg yolks
½ pound dates cut in small pieces
1 cup English walnuts (chopped)
3 egg whites beaten until stiff (not dry)

Mix together sugar, flour, baking powder and salt.
Gradually add beaten egg yolks.
Then add chopped dates and English walnuts.
Finally fold in beaten egg whites.
Turn into 9 x 9 inch greased pan.
Bake about 30 minutes in 350 degree oven.
When cool, cut into squares or rectangles.

I generally double this recipe.
Dust with 10x sugar if desired.

SOUR CREAM POUND CAKE
YIELDS 24-26 SERVINGS

3 cups sugar
2 sticks butter
6 eggs
1 cup sour cream
1 teaspoon vanilla
3 cups flour
¼ teaspoon salt
¼ teaspoon baking soda

Cream together butter and sugar.
Add eggs one at a time.
Add sour cream and vanilla.
Scrape bottom and side of mixing bowl.
Gradually add flour, salt, and baking soda,
which has been sifted together.
Scrape bowl again and mix well.
Grease and flour tube pan.
Bake at 325 degree for about 1½ hours.

Test to be sure cake is done. Remove from oven and
turn cake upside down and let cake cool in pan.
When cold remove from pan and dust
with Confectioner's sugar.

COCONUT CHERRY COOKIES
YIELDS ABOUT 60-65 COOKIES

2½ cups cake flour
1 teaspoon baking powder
1 teaspoon salt
1 cup butter
1 cup sugar
1 teaspoon almond extract
2 eggs
2 cups Angel Flake coconut
½ cup Maraschino Cherries (cut into small bits)
1 cup chopped English walnuts

Sift together flour, baking powder and salt.
Beat butter and sugar until fluffy. Add almond extract.
Add flour mixture to eggs, butter, sugar and almond extract.
Mix well and fold in coconut and chopped walnuts.
Drop mixture by teaspoonful onto greased cooking sheet.

Press several cherry bits onto each cookie,
or if you prefer, they may be folded into the cookie mixture.

Bake at 350 degrees about 10 minutes
or until just lightly browned.

149

CARROT CAKE
YIELDS 20-24 SERVINGS

2 cups sugar
3 cups whole wheat flour
1 teaspoon baking powder
1 teaspoon baking soda
½ teaspoon salt
1 cup Crisco oil
4 eggs beaten
3 cups grated carrots
½ cup chopped pecans
½ cup raisins
½ cup chopped dates
1 cup crushed pineapple
1 cup mashed bananas
½ cup Angel Flake Coconut
1 teaspoon vanilla
1 teaspoon cinnamon

Measure sugar, wheat flour, baking powder, baking soda,
salt, vanilla, and cinnamon into large bowl.
In another large bowl, put grated carrots, pecans,
raisins, dates, crushed pineapple, coconut and bananas.
In mixer beat eggs and oil together and then add
the rest of the ingredients a small amount at a time,
alternately the dry ingredients and the carrots, fruit, and nuts.
Mix together well and bake in tube pan,
deep sheet pan 14 x 10 x 2 inch, or small loaf pans.
Bake at 325 degrees about 1 hour, ten minutes or
until tooth pick comes out clean.
A cream cheese icing is very good with this cake.

ORANGE BLOSSOMS
MAKES ABOUT 85

*1 recipe of your favorite white cake
or one box white cake mix
grated rind and juice of 2 medium size oranges
grated rind and juice of 2 medium size lemons
granulated sugar enough to make a thick glaze*

Follow recipe for white cake (either box or your own).
Fill tiny greased and floured muffin tins ⅔ full.
Bake in 350 degree oven for 10 to 12 minutes.
Turn out onto paper towels.
Make glaze of sugar, orange and lemon rind and juices.
Dip tops of tiny cakes and return to paper towels
while they are still slightly warm. Allow them to cool.
Store in closed container in freezer and use as needed.

151

MOCK LADY BALTIMORE CAKE
YIELDS 2 (9 IN.) LAYERS

1 recipe your favorite white cake or mix
7 minute frosting
butter cream frosting
white decorator frosting or
sweetened whipped cream

Filling
½ cup chopped candied or maraschino cherries
½ cup chopped pecans
½ cup chopped pitted dates
½ cup chopped figs
½ cup snipped white raisins or
candied pineapple

Bake cake according to recipe directions.
Mix together chopped fruits and nuts
and blend them with about one forth of your frosting.
Spread fruit between cake layers.
I put just a little round of the fruit mix
in the center of the top layer.
Spread rest of frosting on sides and top of the cake.

I use my Wedding Cake Recipe
(see table of contents)

152

ORANGE CAKE
YIELDS 2 (9 IN.) LAYERS

grated rind of 1 orange
1 ½ cups granulated sugar
¾ cup butter or margarine
3 eggs
3 cups cake flour
¾ teaspoon salt
3 ½ teaspoons baking powder
½ cup orange juice
½ cup water
2 tablespoons fresh squeezed lemon juice

Sift together flour, salt, and baking powder.
Cream together butter, sugar, and orange juice.
Beat in the eggs one at a time.
Measure orange juice, lemon juice and
water into a small pitcher or bowl.
Add flour mixture and juice mixture
alternately to beaten egg sugar etc.
Mixing thoroughly after each addition.
Bake in 2 nine inch cake pans
in a 375 degree oven about 30 minutes.
When cool, frost with orange icing.

Orange Icing
⅓ cup butter or margarine
4 ½ cups confectioner's sugar
¼ cup orange juice
1 ¼ teaspoons grated orange rind

Beat together well until of a spreading consistency.

153

GRANDMA'S OLD FASHIONED SUGAR COOKIES

MAKES ABOUT 50 COOKIES

½ cup shortening
½ cup sugar
1 egg
1 teaspoon vanilla
½ cup sour cream
1 ½ cups cake flour
1 teaspoon baking powder
½ teaspoon baking soda
¾ teaspoon salt
large seeded raisins

Cream shortening and sugar together.
Combine egg, vanilla, and sour cream together.
Sift together cake flour, baking powder, baking soda, and salt.
Add egg, vanilla and sour cream mixture, alternately
with flour mixture to shortening and sugar mixture.
Beat well after each addition. Chill dough well.

Roll out on lightly floured board to a scant ¼ inch,
then cut with a large cookie cutter,
about 2 to 2½ inch in diameter.
Sprinkle cookies with sugar and gently press sugar into cookies.
Press 1 seeded raisin into each cookie. Bake at 375 degree
for about 12 to 15 minutes.
Recipe may be doubled.

With a glass of cold milk
they are a great after-school snack.

154

APPLESAUCE RAISIN COOKIES
MAKES ABOUT 5½ DOZEN COOKIES

¾ cup Crisco
1 cup light brown sugar, firmly packed
1 egg
½ cup applesauce
2¼ cups sifted flour, plus 1½ tablespoons
½ teaspoon soda
½ teaspoon salt
¾ teaspoon ground cinnamon
¼ teaspoon ground cloves
1 cup seedless raisins
½ cup chopped pecans
1 teaspoon vanilla

Beat together Crisco and brown sugar until fluffy.
Add egg and beat well.
Stir in applesauce.
Sift dry ingredients and mix well.
Fold in raisins and nuts.
Drop by teaspoon full onto greased cookie sheet.
Bake in 370 degree oven 10-12 minutes.

155

ELEANOR'S GINGER COOKIES
YIELDS ABOUT 80 COOKIES

2 cups sugar
1½ cups Crisco
½ teaspoon salt
2 eggs
½ cup Br'er Rabbit molasses (dark)
4 teaspoons baking soda
4 cups flour
2 teaspoons ground cinnamon
1 teaspoon ground ginger
¾ teaspoon ground cloves
granulated sugar

Sift together flour, soda, salt, cinnamon, ginger and cloves.
Cream sugar and shortening well.
Add eggs and molasses and mix well.
Add dry ingredients, flour etc. and thoroughly blend.
Chill well.
Roll dough into small balls, about ¾ inch.
Roll balls in granulated sugar.
Bake on greased cookie sheet about 10 minutes,
in 375 degree oven.

DATE AND NUT BARS
YIELDS 40 - 45 BARS

1 cup sugar
3 eggs
2 cups chopped dates
1 cup chopped pecans
1 scant cup flour
1 teaspoon baking powder
⅛ teaspoon salt
¼ teaspoon ground cloves
¼ teaspoon ground cinnamon
1 teaspoon vanilla

Beat eggs until very light, add sugar slowly.
Continue beating until they are light and fluffy.
Add dates and nuts, blend well.
Sift together flour, baking powder, salt and spices.
Add vanilla to egg mixture.
Add flour mixture to egg mixture. Blend all thoroughly.
Grease and line with wax paper a 9 x 13 inch pan and fill with dough.
Spread batter evenly in the pan.
Bake in moderate 325 degree oven for about 25 minutes.
Turn out on cookie sheet, remove wax paper and let cool.
When cake is cold, cut into 1 x 1½ inch bars.
Roll in confectioners sugar.
Store in cool place.

157

APPLESAUCE CAKE
YIELDS ABOUT 20 SERVINGS

4 cups flour
2 eggs
1 cup butter or margarine
3 teaspoons baking soda
1 teaspoon salt
1 cup raisins
2 cups sugar
1½ teaspoons ground cinnamon
2 cups chopped nuts
2 cups apple sauce
2 teaspoons vanilla

Cream together butter or margarine
and sugar, add eggs, and beat well.
Sift together flour, cinnamon,
baking soda and salt.
Add vanilla to apple sauce and mix
alternately with flour mixture.
Scrape sides of mixing bowl and mix until
all is blended well, fold in raisins and nuts.
Pour into well greased and floured tube pan.
Bake in 350 degree oven about 80 minutes,
testing with pick for doneness.
Store in cool place.

158

COFFEE CAKE SUPREME
YIELDS 24 PIECES

½ cup butter or margarine
1 cup sugar
2 eggs
1 cup commercial sour cream
1 teaspoon vanilla
2 cups all purpose flour
1 teaspoon baking powder
1 teaspoon soda

Sprinkle Mix
¼ cup sugar
1 teaspoon ground cinnamon
½ cup white raisins

Cream together butter and sugar, beat in eggs,
one at a time and add sour cream and vanilla
to batter, and mix the flour, baking powder
and soda which have been sifted together several times.
Spread half the batter in a buttered
9 x 12 x 3 inch Pyrex baking dish.

Sprinkle with the cinnamon, sugar and raisin mixture.

Carefully spread the remaining batter over the sugar mixture.
Use a small flat spatula to spread carefully.

Top with the following mixture for the topping.
Mix together ¼ cup light brown sugar, 1 tablespoon flour,
½ teaspoon ground cinnamon and ⅓ cup chopped pecans.

Drizzle about 2½ tablespoons melted butter over top.
Bake at 325 degrees about 40 minutes.

Recipe may be doubled, excellent for brunch.

159

MY WEDDING CAKE
YIELDS 2 (9 INCH) LAYERS

1 cup granulated sugar
¼ cup butter or margarine
¼ cup Crisco
6 egg whites (extra large eggs)
2 cups cake flour (sifted)
3 teaspoons baking powder
¼ teaspoon salt
¾ cup milk
1 teaspoon vanilla extract
½ teaspoon almond extract
¼ extra cup sugar (for egg whites)

Sift together flour, baking powder and salt.
Break egg whites into separate bowl.
Yolks may be used elsewhere if stored
tightly covered in refrigerator.
Cream butter and Crisco add sugar slowly and
beat until mixture is light and fluffy.
Add salt and flavorings to milk and alternating
milk and flour mixture a little at a time
beating well after each addition.
In a separate bowl beat egg whites on high speed,
adding the ¼ cup sugar a little at a time until
the egg whites have a soft peak but are not dry.
Carefully fold egg whites in to cake batter
until thoroughly blended.
Pour into a greased and floured cake pan or pans.
Bake at 350 degrees until cake tests done,
about 25-30 minutes for 2 (9 inch) cake pans.

HINTS FOR
"MY WEDDING CAKE" RECIPE

1 recipe makes two 9 x 1½ inch round cakes
2 recipes make one 7½ x 2½ inch round
plus one 10 x 2½ inch round cake for the
top and middle tier of a 3 tier cake.
For the bottom tier of a 3 tier cake, I bake two
(1½ recipes) in a 13 inch round pan and put
them together to form the bottom tier.
The tiers are then iced and decorated to suit the
occasion be it wedding, birthday, or anniversary,
use a bit of food coloring in some of the decorations
to suit the occasion.

This same recipe may also be baked in a
shallow (jelly roll) pan, and iced and cut into
rectangles, squares or diamond shape and
decorated in pastel colors
for teas, showers, parties, etc..

RED VELVET CAKE
YIELDS 2 (9 INCH) LAYERS

½ cup Crisco shortening
1½ cups granulated sugar
2 eggs
2 tablespoons cocoa
2 ounces red food coloring
1 teaspoon salt
1 teaspoon vanilla
1 cup butter-milk
1½ teaspoons baking soda
2½ cups flour
1 tablespoon vinegar

Measure sugar into a small bowl, and measure flour in a bowl.
Measure butter-milk and put into a small pitcher and
add salt and vanilla and stir.
Into another container put the cocoa and
red food coloring and mix well.
In one small cup put the vinegar and in another the baking soda.
Put shortening and sugar in mixing bowl
and beat until it is very light and fluffy.
Add the eggs and beat well.
Next add the dissolved coca and food coloring.
When blended well, add, alternating the flour
and buttermilk, vanilla and salt, mixing well after each
addition, scraping sides and bottom of the bowl often.
All additions should be mixed slowly so as not to splash.
When completely mixed remove bowl from mixer.
Pour vinegar over the soda and mix well and
fold into cake dough immediately.
Blend completely but do not beat.
Pour into 2 (9-inch) cake pans
and bake at 350 degrees or until done.

I can't emphasize how important the thorough blending and
careful folding is. If not blended right the cake will have
streaks and your counter will be a mess.

162

APPLESAUCE CAKE ROLL
MAKES 15-16 SLICES

3 eggs
¾ cup granulated sugar
1 cup applesauce
1 cup all purpose flour
½ teaspoon baking powder
½ teaspoon baking soda
½ teaspoon ground cinnamon
¼ teaspoon ground cloves
¼ teaspoon salt
powdered sugar
½ cup chopped English walnuts
1 cup whipping cream

Beat eggs until they are thick adding sugar gradually,
scrapping sides of bowl often.
Sift together the flour, baking powder, baking soda,
cinnamon, and salt.
Add ½ cup applesauce and flour mixture alternately
until all has been blended together well.
Pour batter into a greased and floured
15 x 10 x 1 inch jelly roll pan.
Bake at 350 degrees about 10-20 minutes.
When done turn out onto towel which
has been sprinkled with powdered sugar.
Roll up and let cool on rack.
When cold, whip cream until light and will peak softly.
Add the rest of the applesauce and chopped nuts.
Spread cake roll evenly and roll up immediately.
Sprinkle with 10x sugar if desired.
Chill and slice ⅔ inch slices to serve.

163

OLD FASHIONED SAND TARTS
MAKES 75-80 COOKIES

2 cups sifted cake flour
½ cup butter, real butter only
1 cup sugar
1 egg well beaten
1½ teaspoon baking powder
1 teaspoon vanilla
1 slightly beaten egg white
¼ teaspoon cinnamon
2 tablespoons sugar
1 cup blanched almonds split in half

Beat together, creaming well, the cup
of sugar, butter, and egg.
Add flour and baking powder which
has been sifted together. Add vanilla.
Mix well and place in refrigerator to chill.
Mix the 2 tablespoons sugar and cinnamon together.
Grease cookie sheet. On lightly floured board roll a small
portion of the cookie dough until it is very thin.
Cut cookies with 2½ inch cutter.
Place on cookie sheet about 1 inch apart.
Brush with beaten egg white, sprinkle
on cinnamon, sugar. Place 1 half of almond into the
center of each cookie. Bake in 375 degree oven
for about 7 minutes.
Watch carefully as they burn easily.

ELEGANT PECAN PUFFS
YIELDS ABOUT 32

½ cup butter
2 tablespoons sugar
1 teaspoon vanilla
1 cup flour
1 cup pecans, measure then grind
confectioners sugar

Beat butter until soft.
Add sugar and blend until creamy,
Add vanilla.
Stir in flour and ground pecans,
mix well and chill.
Roll dough into 1 inch balls.
Place on greased cookie sheet.
Bake in slow oven, 300 degrees
for about 45 minutes.
Roll in confectioners sugar while still hot.
When cold roll again in confectioners sugar.
They are very rich.

Recipe may be doubled.

165

OLD FASHIONED GINGER SNAPS
YIELDS ABOUT 40 COOKIES

½ cup brown sugar
½ cup shortening
1 medium sized egg
½ cup dark molasses
½ tablespoon vinegar
2 cups sifted flour
½ teaspoon soda
½ teaspoon salt
2 teaspoons ground ginger
¼ teaspoon ground cinnamon (optional)
¼ teaspoon ground cloves (optional)

Sift together sifted flour, salt, soda and spices.
Beat shortening and sugar until fluffy.
Add egg, molasses and vinegar.
Blend flour and sugar mixture together and mix well.
On floured board roll dough very thin.
Cut into rounds with 1½ inch cutter.
Bake in moderate oven, 350 degrees
for about 8 minutes.
Recipe may be doubled. In that case
one extra large egg is sufficient.

MERINGUE NUT KISSES
YIELDS ABOUT 65 KISSES

3 extra large egg whites
1⅓ cups granulated sugar
1½ teaspoon vanilla
1 cup chopped pecans
pink or green food coloring (optional)

Have egg whites at room temperature.
Beat them in mixer until they will hold a soft peak.
Add sugar very gradually beating continuously.
Scrape sides of mixing bowl and fold
in vanilla and food coloring.
Return to bowl and blend well.
Remove bowl and fold in pecans.
Drop onto a wax paper covered cookie sheet.
Shape into little cones.
Bake in a very slow oven (225 degrees) until
they are firm and dry.
Remove from wax paper promptly.

167

Luscious Applesauce Bread
YIELDS 30 SLICES

1 ¼ cups applesauce
1 cup granulated sugar
3 tablespoons milk
½ cup cooking oil
2 eggs
2 cups all purpose flour
1 teaspoon baking soda
1 ½ teaspoon baking powder
½ teaspoon salt
¼ teaspoon ground nutmeg
½ teaspoon ground cinnamon
¼ teaspoon allspice
½ cup chopped pecans
½ cup seedless raisins (optional)

Topping
¼ cup chopped pecans
¼ cup light brown sugar
½ teaspoon ground cinnamon

In mixer combine applesauce, sugar, oil, eggs and milk.
Sift together flour, soda, baking powder,
cinnamon, nutmeg and allspice.
Slowly blend together the flour mixture into the applesauce mix.
Fold in chopped pecans and raisins.
Turn into 3 (9 x 5 x 3 inch) loaf pans.
Combine topping ingredients, mix well
and sprinkle over each pan.
Bake at 350 degrees about 35-40 minutes.

I sometimes bake it in tiny loaf pans. They make a lovely
little gift. Securely wrapped, they freeze beautifully
and are great if a neighbor or friend drops in
for a cup of coffee or tea.

168

ERMINE ICING
YIELDS 2½ CUPS

3 tablespoons sifted flour
1 teaspoon vanilla
1 cup milk
1 cup granulated sugar
1 cup butter or margarine

Cook blended flour and milk until thick, stirring constantly.
Remove from stove and let it cool until it is cold.
Beat into the cold flour mixture, the sugar,
butter, and vanilla.
Beat until the icing is of spreading consistency.
Enough for 2 nine inch layers.

This icing is especially good on Red Velvet Cake.

CREAM CHEESE FROSTING

6 oz. cream cheese
½ cup butter
2 teaspoons vanilla
4½ to 4¾ cups confectioners sugar

In mixer beat together cream cheese, butter,
and vanilla until it is light and fluffy.
Add 2 cups confectioners sugar slowing until well mixed.
Gradually add confectioners sugar until frosting is
of the right consistency to spread.
Frost cake and store in a cool place or cover
and place in refrigerator.
Will frost tops and sides of 2 (8-9 inch) layers.

This frosting is good on Red Velvet cake,
Carrot cake and Spice cake

169

Pies & Puddings

171

CHEESE CAKE PIE
SERVES 8

1 graham cracker crust
1 (8-oz.) package cream cheese
1 cup 10x sugar (packed)
1 teaspoon vanilla
1 teaspoon lemon juice
8 oz. container Cool Whip
cherry or blueberry pie filling

Prepare crust according to package.
I bake the crust about 8-10 minutes
ahead and allow it to cool.
Beat cream cheese, add vanilla and lemon juice,
slowly add 10x sugar and mix all well.
Slowly blend in Cool Whip.
Turn into cooled shell.
Top with cherry or blueberry filling if desired.
I prefer to top each pie serving
with the topping as it is served.

172

SWEET POTATO PIE
SERVES 8

1 recipe plain pastry
1¾ cups mashed sweet potatoes
2 tablespoons melted butter
⅔ cup light brown sugar
1 teaspoon ground cinnamon
½ teaspoon ground nutmeg
½ teaspoon salt
2 beaten eggs
1¾ cups rich milk
2 tablespoons cream sherry (optional)
⅔ cup broken pecan meats

Line 9 inch pie pan with pastry.
In mixing bowl combine all ingredients in
the order they are listed, fold in the pecans last.
Pour into pie pan shell and cover with
lattice pastry or diamond shapes of pastry.
Bake at 450 degrees for 10 minutes
Reduce heat to 350 degrees and bake about 45 minutes
or until knife comes out clean.

You can omit the sherry and add
½ cup orange juice instead.
You can omit the pastry topping for the pie and
just sprinkle the chopped nuts around the edge
of the pie instead of putting them in
the sweet potato mixture.

173

GREEN TOMATO PIE
SERVES 8

1 recipe pie dough (plain)
3 cups sliced green tomatoes
1⅓ cups sugar
3 tablespoons flour
¼ teaspoon salt
6 tablespoons lemon juice
4 teaspoons grated lemon rind
4 tablespoons butter
¾ teaspoon ground cinnamon

Combine sliced tomatoes, (they need not be peeled),
sugar, flour, lemon juice and lemon rind and salt.
Line pie pan with crust. Pour in filling,
dot with butter. Cover with top crust
which has been slashed with small vents to
allow steam to escape. Crimp edges of pie.
Bake in a 450 degree oven for 10 minutes.
Reduce heat to 350 degrees and bake another 30-35 minutes,
until lightly browned or until the tomatoes are tender.

You may want to omit top crust and
substitute a crumb topping.

Crumb Topping
2 tablespoons flour
1/3 cup light brown sugar
2 tablespoons melted butter
1/3 teaspoon ground cinnamon

Blend all together and sprinkle over top of pie.
Bake the same as you would with the double crust.

174

QUICHE LORRAINE
SERVES 8

1 unbaked pie shell (9 inch)
½ lb. grated Swiss cheese
1½ tablespoons flour
8 slices bacon
3 slightly beaten eggs
2 tablespoons grated or finely minced onion
1¼ cups half and half milk
½ teaspoon salt
¼ teaspoon pepper

Cook bacon in skillet until crisp: drain and crumble.
Reserve a couple tablespoons of bacon for top
of pie. Place remaining bacon in pie, add cheese and
flour which has been mixed together. Mix other ingredients
together and pour into shell. Trim with the rest of the bacon.
I sometimes add about ⅓ cup finely chopped green peppers
to the milk mixture. Bake at 400 degrees for about 12
minutes then reduce oven heat to 300 degrees and
bake for about 35 to 40 minutes longer or until
an inserted knife comes out clean.

This recipe can be used for tiny mini tarts, but then
I put onion, bacon, milk in processor until well
blended. Then combine that with beaten eggs,
the grated cheese, flour, seasonings and spoon into
mini-tart shells and bake at 325 degrees for
about 40 minutes.

APPLE PIE
SERVES 6-8

Pastry Dough
2 cups flour
1 cup Crisco
1 teaspoon salt
1 egg and ice cold water enough to fill 1 cup
a little more water may be needed.

Filling
5 or 6 medium sized apples- I prefer (Rome Beauty or Stayman)
¾ to 1 cup sugar (depending on tartness of apples)
1 teaspoon ground cinnamon
2 tablespoons flour
¼ teaspoon salt
1½ tablespoons butter

Blend together pastry ingredients,
handling no more than necessary.
Peel, core, and thinly slice apples.
Mix together sugar, cinnamon, salt, and flour.
Combine sugar etc. with apples.
Using about ½ dough roll out on floured board,
the bottom crust.
Cover bottom of pie pan with bottom crust
(moisten edges of crust)
Fill with apple mixture. Dot with butter.
Roll out top crust, cut several openings in crust.
Cover pie with top crust. Sprinkle with sugar.
Secure and crimp crust with fork or fingers.
Place in heated oven 425 degrees. Bake about 15 minutes,
reduce heat to 350 degrees and continue to bake about
45 minutes or until done.

CHERRY CHEESE CAKE PIE
SERVES 8

1 ½ cups Graham cracker crumbs
¼ cup sugar
⅓ cup softened margarine
8 oz. Cream cheese (room temperature)
1 cup 10x sugar
8 oz. Cool Whip
1 teaspoon Vanilla
1 ½ teaspoon lemon juice
Cherry Pie Filling
½ teaspoon almond extract

To prepare pie crust (9 inch) blend Graham cracker
crumbs, ¼ cup sugar and ⅓ cup softened margarine,
mix until it is well blended. Carefully press into pie pan.
Bake crust about 8 or 9 minutes in a 350 degree oven. Cool.
Beat cream cheese well, add lemon juice and vanilla, slowly
blend in 10x sugar, continue mixing, scraping sides
and bottom of mixing bowl several times. Slowly, blend
in Cool Whip. Turn mixture into pie shell and spread evenly.
Top with cherries to which you have added the almond extract.
I prefer to spoon the cherries onto the cut slices of
the pie after they are placed on their serving plate.
It is a little neater. I think Blueberry filling is also very
nice to use instead of the cherries.

* Keep pie in the refrigerator until ready to serve.

GRAHAM CRACKER PIE
SERVES 6-8

2½ cups Graham Cracker crumbs
½ cup sugar
⅔ cup softened margarine

Mix all together thoroughly. Line bottom of pie pan
with ½ crumbs, bake for about 6 minutes in 350 degree oven.
Set rest of crumbs aside for topping.

Custard Filling
3 egg yolks
⅓ cup sugar
¼ teaspoon salt
2½ tablespoons corn starch
1 tablespoon butter
2 cups scalded milk

Beat egg yolks, gradually beating in sugar, salt, corn starch, butter.
Pour over these ingredients, the scalded milk.
Cook and continue to stir over boiling water on very low heat.
Stir constantly until it thickens, remove from heat, and
add vanilla. Pour into pie shell and top with meringue.

Meringue
3 egg whites
1 tablespoon water
¼ teaspoon cream of tartar
6 tablespoons sugar
¾ teaspoon vanilla

Beat egg whites, cream of tarter and water in small bowl
at high speed about 3 minutes. Add sugar gradually, add salt and
vanilla. Continue beating on high speed until mixture will stand
in peaks. Cover filled pie shell, spreading meringue lightly with
knife or spatula. Cover with remaining graham crumbs. Bake in
300 degree oven about 20 minutes.
Remove pie and let it cool gradually.

Rolls & Breads

MRS TOMS' ROLLS
MAKES 5 DOZEN ROLLS

2 eggs
1 cup water
2 packages active dry yeast
1⅓ cups milk (scalded)
2 tablespoons sugar
2 tablespoons Crisco
1½ teaspoons salt
1 extra tablespoon sugar
about 1¾ pounds Gold Medal Wondra flour

Break eggs into mixer bowl, add 1 cup water.
Measure 2 tablespoons sugar, Crisco and salt into
another bowl and pour the hot scalded milk over it.
Beat eggs and water and add about ⅓ of the
milk mixture over eggs and water in mixer.
When lukewarm add yeast and 1 tablespoon of sugar.
Mix thoroughly. When the other ⅔ of the milk is lukewarm,
add to eggs etc. and begin beating in the flour a small amount
at a time. Continue adding the flour and mixing until dough
seems stiff enough to handle. Turn dough out on floured board
and with care, work dough into a soft ball.
Return dough into bowl, grease top lightly with melted Crisco.
Cover and set in warm place to rise. When doubled in bulk,
punch down dough and using greased hands,
squeeze out 1 inch little balls of dough between
your thumb and fore finger.
Place little rolls on a greased baking sheet and
let them rise until doubled in size.
Bake at 375 degree for 10-12 minutes.

Never allow your dough to get too warm or too cold.
Just nice and warm.
This recipe maybe used for cinnamon buns and sticky buns.
See recipes in this book.

MRS TOMS' CINNAMON ROLLS
YIELDS ABOUT 3 DOZEN

1 Mrs Toms' Roll Recipe
melted butter
¾ cup sugar
3 tablespoons ground cinnamon

Glaze
1 cup 10x sugar
3 tablespoons warm milk
½ teaspoon vanilla

This glaze recipe is enough for 1 dozen cinnamon rolls.
Double or triple if necessary

Roll ⅓ of roll recipe into a 9 x 13 inch square ½ inch thick.
Brush with melted butter.
Sprinkle generously with cinnamon sugar mix.
Roll up as you would a jelly roll.
Cut into 12 slices one inch wide and place
in a 9 x 13 x 2 inch buttered pan.
Allow space between each roll to rise. Repeat the procedure.
Brush tops and sides of rolls with butter.
Set in warm place to rise, when doubled in bulk,
bake in a 375 degree oven until light brown
and done, about 20-25 minutes.
Remove from oven. Repeat process with remaining dough.
Beat together 10x sugar, warm milk and vanilla
and spread over cooled buns,
or add a bit more warm milk and drizzle over buns.

You may wish to use ½ roll recipe to make into rolls
and the other half to make cinnamon buns
or sticky buns.

181

MRS. TOMS' STICKY BUNS
MAKES ABOUT 3½ DOZEN BUNS

1 recipe Mrs. Toms' Rolls
ground cinnamon
4 cups brown sugar
2 cups butter or margarine
1½ cups seedless raisins
1½ cups chopped pecans
melted butter to brush buns

Beat together butter and brown sugar.
Spread generously in bottom of 9 x 12 x 3 inch pan.
The above recipe will do three pans.
Sprinkle generously with pecans and seedless raisins.
Roll ⅓ dough into a 9 x 13 inch rectangle.
Brush dough with butter or margarine.
Sprinkle with cinnamon, a few pecans and a few raisins.
Roll up as you would a jelly roll.
Cut the roll into 12 one inch wide slices
and put them into baking pan.
Allow some space between each bun for expansion.
Let rise until double in bulk.
Bake in 375 degree oven until light brown
on top and sugar and nut mix is syrupy.
Line tray or other container or pan with wax paper
and sprinkle lightly with 10x sugar.
Turn pan with buns upside down onto
tray or other container or pan, so that
the pecans, raisins, etc will be on top.
Repeat with rest of dough or make rolls with the rest.

The rolls will freeze beautifully.

182

DELECTABLE DOUGHNUTS
MAKES ABOUT 36 DOUGHNUTS

4¼ cups sifted flour
4 teaspoons baking powder
¾ teaspoon ground nutmeg
½ teaspoon salt
2 eggs
1 cup sugar
2 tablespoons melted butter
1 cup milk
1 teaspoon vanilla
sugar or confectioners sugar or cinnamon sugar

Sift together dry ingredients.
Beat eggs and add sugar gradually until light.
Stir in melted butter, milk and vanilla.
Add dry ingredients stirring until batter is smooth.
Knead the dough on lightly floured board.
Roll out to ⅜ inch thickness.
Cut with floured doughnut cutter.
Fry in deep hot oil 370 degrees, turning once.
Drain on paper towels.
Roll doughnuts in regular Confectioners,
or cinnamon sugar.

183

PUMPKIN BREAD DELUXE
MAKES 55-60 SLICES

1 cup Crisco oil
⅔ cup water
3½ cups sifted flour
2 teaspoons baking soda
1½ cups granulated sugar
4 eggs beaten
2 cups canned pumpkin
1½ teaspoons salt
1 teaspoon ground nutmeg
1 teaspoon ground cinnamon
1 teaspoon vanilla
1½ cups light brown sugar
1 cup white raisins
½ cup chopped pecans
½ cup chopped black walnuts

Sift flour, soda, spices and baking soda.
Beat eggs lightly, mix in Crisco oil, water, and pumpkin.
Blend all together well, add vanilla.
Gradually add flour mixture a small amount at a time,
alternating with the granulated sugar and the brown sugar.
Fold in the raisins and nuts.
Pour into greased and floured (5½ x 3½ inch) loaf pans.
Bake in 350 degree oven about one hour or
until wooden pick comes out clean.
Makes about 6 pans that will slice 10-11 slices each.

Excellent for parties or the holidays as they freeze well.

BAKING POWDER BISCUITS
MAKES 12-14 (2 INCH) BISCUITS

2 cups sifted flour
2 teaspoons baking powder
4 tablespoons butter or Crisco
1/2 teaspoon salt
3/4 cup milk

Measure the sifted flour, add the baking powder
and salt and sift again.
Cut in butter or Crisco until well mixed.
Gradually add the milk stirring until
it becomes a soft dough.
Take ½ of the dough and put it on a lightly floured board.
Knead dough quickly until it becomes a nice soft ball.
Roll to about ½ inch thickness.
Cut with a 2 inch biscuit cutter, dip cutter in
flour each time so the dough doesn't stick.
For smaller biscuits use a 1¼ or 1½ inch cutter.
Repeat with rest of dough.
Bake in a 450 degree oven until biscuits are
lightly browned, about 12-15 minutes.

QUICK DROP BISCUITS
MAKES 18-20 BISCUITS

2 cups sifted flour
2 teaspoons baking powder
4 tablespoons butter or Crisco shortening
½ teaspoon salt
1 cup milk minus 1 tablespoon

Measure the flour which has already been sifted once,
add the baking powder and salt.
Cut in the butter or Crisco until mixed very well.
Gradually add milk until dough becomes a soft ball.
Drop by teaspoon onto ungreased baking sheet.
Bake in 450 degree oven until biscuits are
lightly browned.

Add 1 cup grated American cheese with the shortening
for cheese biscuits. Makes 18-20.

OLD FASHIONED PUMPKIN BREAD

3 eggs slightly beaten
3 cups sugar
1 cup Mazola or Crisco oil
2 cups prepared pumpkin
3 cups all purpose flour
1 teaspoon baking soda
½ teaspoon baking powder
1 teaspoon ground nutmeg
1 teaspoon ground cinnamon
½ teaspoon ground cloves
½ teaspoon salt
1 teaspoon vanilla

Grease and flour small (5½ x 3½ inch) loaf pans.
Sift together flour, baking soda,
baking powder, salt and spices.
Beat eggs add sugar, a little at a time until light and fluffy.
Add Mazola or Crisco oil and vanilla.
Slowly add flour mixture until all is well blended.
Pour into loaf pans, bake in 350 degree oven
about 50 minutes or until they test done.
When cold, they may be frosted with
cream cheese icing if desired.

They freeze well.

Sauces & Dressings

189

HOT FUDGE SAUCE
MAKES ABOUT 1 CUP OF SAUCE

1 tablespoon butter
1 square (1 oz.) unsweetened chocolate
½ cup boiling water
1 cup granulated sugar
2 tablespoons light corn syrup
½ teaspoon vanilla
⅛ teaspoon salt

Melt butter, add chocolate and stir over a very
low heat until chocolate melts.
Add boiling water gradually, stirring constantly
until it begins to boil.
Add sugar and corn syrup, stirring until
all is dissolved. Simmer about 5 minutes.
Add vanilla and salt.

A couple scoops vanilla ice cream,
a couple chopped nuts, Hot Fudge Sundae!

190

MARSHMALLOW SAUCE
MAKES 2½ CUPS

1 cup sugar
½ cup water
16 marshmallows
2 egg whites

Cut marshmallows into small pieces.
Bring water and sugar to a boil and boil about 5 minutes.
Add marshmallows to hot syrup, cool and stir
until marshmallows are completely dissolved.
Pour mixture over stiffly beaten egg whites,
beat until smooth.
Flavor with mint or vanilla if desired.
Add a few snipped marshmallows
just before serving if desired.

SALAD GREENS DRESSING
MAKES ABOUT 2 CUPS

1 cup mayonnaise
½ cup sour cream
2 tablespoons minced onion or chives
3 tablespoons wine vinegar
1 tablespoon lemon juice
1 clove mashed or grated garlic
salt and pepper to taste

Combine all ingredients and chill.
The dressing thickens on standing.

For a milder dressing, omit the wine vinegar.
The dressing is excellent for raw vegetables.

CREAMY FRUIT DRESSING
YIELDS 1½ CUPS

1 (8-oz.) package cream cheese
½ cup fresh squeezed orange juice
¼ teaspoon salt
¼ teaspoon almond extract
3 tablespoons sugar

Beat cream cheese with sugar.
Add other ingredients and mix well.
This is good with fresh fruit, strawberries,
blueberries, peaches, nectarines etc.

Special Recipes

Joan's Corn Pudding
YIELDS 12-15 SERVINGS

3 cups whole grain sweet corn
6 eggs beaten
2 tablespoons butter
6 tablespoons sugar
3 teaspoons corn starch
1 teaspoon salt
2⅔ cups milk

Beat eggs well add other ingredients
and mix well add corn last.
Pour into buttered 3-quart casserole.
Bake immediately in 350 degree oven for 50-60 minutes.
For a lesser quantity divide recipe in half.

My daughter buys fresh sweet corn in the summer
and freezes it in small containers.
She then is able, through out the year, to
make the best corn pudding ever.

Daughter, Joan Derrick

JOAN'S SUGAR COOKIES
YIELDS ABOUT 60-70 COOKIES

½ cup butter
1½ cups sugar
1/4 cup milk
2 eggs
½ teaspoon vanilla
½ teaspoon ground nutmeg
½ teaspoon salt
2½ teaspoons baking powder
3½ cups flour
plain or lightly colored sugar

Sift flour, nutmeg, salt and baking powder together.
Cream butter and sugar well.
Beat eggs and vanilla.
Mix well and chill well.
Roll out on floured board until very thin.
Cut with cookie cutters and place on
lightly greased cookie sheet.
Sprinkle lightly with white or lightly
colored (pink or green) sugar.
Bake at 375 degrees for about 9 minutes.

The cookie cutters, may be round,
stars, bells, rabbits etc..

Daughter, Joan Derrick

JOAN'S MUSHROOM SCALLOPED POTATOES
YIELDS 6-8 SERVINGS

1 (10-oz.) can cream of mushroom soup
grated sharp cheddar cheese
¼ cup dried pimento
½ teaspoon salt
1 (4-oz) can sliced mushrooms (drained)
1 small can Pet milk (evaporated)
4 cups thinly sliced potatoes

Mix soup, ½ cup grated cheese, pimento,
salt and sliced mushrooms.
Stir in Pet milk and potatoes.
Pour into 8 inch round casserole.
Top generously with grated cheese.
Bake at 350 degrees about 1 hour and 15 minutes
or until potatoes are done.

Recipe may be doubled and put into 9 x 13 inch casserole
to bake. Yields approximately 15 servings.

Daughter, Joan Derrick

JOAN'S ESCALLOPED OYSTERS
YIELDS 6-8 SERVINGS

1 quart oysters (drained thoroughly)
reserve liquid from oysters
1 cup bread crumbs
1½ cups cracker crumbs (saltines)
1 cup melted butter
cream
salt and pepper to taste

Mix crumbs and butter, salt and pepper.
Put a thin layer of crumbs in a buttered baking dish.
Cover with half the oysters.
Add 2 tablespoons oyster liquid and 2 tablespoons cream.
Repeat with few crumbs, then oysters,
then oyster liquid and cream.
Top with remaining crumbs.
Bake 30 minutes in 425 degree oven being
careful not to scorch the top.

Daughter, Joan Derrick

Patricia's Strawberry Parfait Pie
SERVES 6

1 (3-oz.) package strawberry gelatin
1 cup boiling water
1 pint fresh strawberries
2 (8-oz.) cartons strawberry fruit-flavored yogurt
1 pre-baked pie crust or
1 graham cracker crumb crust
1 cup whipping cream (whipped) or Cool Whip to cover pie

Dissolve gelatin in boiling water. Cool to room temperature.
Wash and stem strawberries. Reserve 5 berries for garnish; slice
remaining berries. Gradually blend cooled gelatin into yogurt.
Chill until mixture mounds when dropped from a spoon.
Fold in sliced strawberries.
Spoon into pre-baked pie shell or graham cracker crumb crust.
Chill until set. Cover with whipped cream or Cool Whip.
Garnish with whole strawberries. Delicious!

Daughter, Patricia Ferrell

PATRICIA'S ORANGE SAUCE
YIELDS 1½ CUPS SAUCE

1 cup (½ pint) dairy sour cream
¼ cup orange marmalade
¼ teaspoon salt

Blend ingredients in a glass or stainless steel sauce pan.
Warm slightly over very low heat. Makes 1¼ cups sauce.
Serve baked or broiled chicken ala orange
with this simple sauce. Delicious!

Daughter, Patricia Ferrell

DIANE'S ORANGE SALAD
SERVES 10-12

2 (3-oz.) packages of orange Jell-O
2 cups boiling water
1½ cups of orange juice or cold water
3 cans mandarin oranges
8 oz. can of crushed pineapple
2 cups miniature marshmallows

Mix first five ingredients together and pour into mold.
Put the marshmallows on top of Jell-O in the mold.
Let set to congeal.

Topping
1 cup orange juice
½ cup sugar
2 tablespoons flour
1 egg 2 tablespoons butter
12 oz. container Cool Whip

In a small saucepan combine the sugar, flour, orange juice,
and egg. Heat until boiling while stirring constantly.
Boil one minute. Add butter and stir until melted.
Cool. Fold cooked mixture into Cool Whip.
Spread on top of salad.

Grand-daughter, Diane Kimble

DIANE'S COCONUT CAKE

1 cup butter
2 cups sugar
6 eggs
1 teaspoon soda
dash salt
2¾ cups cake flour
1 teaspoon baking powder
1 cup buttermilk
1 teaspoon vanilla extract
¾ teaspoon coconut flavoring
fresh grated coconut

Cream butter and sugar until perfectly smooth (about 15 minutes).
Add eggs, beating well after each addition.
Sift dry ingredients together and add to creamed mixture
alternately with buttermilk. Stir in vanilla and coconut flavoring.
Bake in three greased and floured round 9 inch layer pans.
Bake at 350 for about 25 minutes or until layers test done.
Cool and frost with Vanilla Butter-Cream Icing.
Cover each frosted layer and top and sides of cake
with the grated coconut.

Vanilla Butter-Cream Icing
1½ cups softened butter
6-8 cups sifted powdered sugar (approximately 1½ to 2 boxes
of 10x sugar)
4-5 tablespoons half & half or milk
1½ teaspoons vanilla extract

Cream butter at medium speed of an electric mixer; gradually add
sugar alternately with half & half, beating until light and fluffy.
Stir in vanilla.

Grand-daughter, Diane Kimble

DEBORAH'S OREO ICE CREAM CAKE
SERVES 10-12

22 Oreo cookies
⅓ cup butter
½ gallon chocolate chip ice cream
1 jar hot fudge sauce
12 oz. Cool Whip

Crush 20 Oreos in food processor; mix with ⅓ cup of softened
butter. Spread in 9 x 13 inch pan. Freeze 20 minutes.
Spread ½ gallon softened chocolate chip ice cream
(or flavor of your choice) over Oreo mixture.
Freeze 20 minutes. Spread 1 jar of hot fudge sauce
over ice cream and freeze. Spread softened Cool Whip
on fudge sauce. Crush 2 Oreos on top and freeze.
(You may add any variations to the layers as you please.
A butterscotch or caramel layer is great
on top of the hot fudge.)

Grand-daughter, Deborah Bissell

DEBORAH'S CURRIED LENTIL-LEEK SOUP
MAKES 6 OR 7 SERVINGS

¾ cup dried lentils

1 (28-oz.) can crushed tomatoes

1 teaspoon curry powder

2 tablespoons chopped fresh basil

¼ teaspoon salt

1/8 teaspoon ground black pepper

1 leek, thinly sliced

2 (14½-oz.) cans fat-free chicken broth

Pre-soaking is not necessary with lentils.
Combine all ingredients in a 3½ quart slow cooker.
Cover and cook on LOW 6½ to 7 hours
or until lentils are tender. Ladle into soup bowls.

Grand-daughter, Deborah Bissell

DEBORAH'S CORNY CORN BREAD
SERVES 12

2 boxes Jiffy Cornbread mix
1 stick margarine
2 eggs
18 oz. sour cream
1 large can cream corn

Melt margarine in a 9 x 13 inch baking pan.
Mix other ingredients well. Pour into the melted margarine.
Swirl the melted margarine around the top of the batter
so it evenly distributes and does not puddle.
Bake at 350 for 30-40 minutes until golden on top.

Grand-daughter, Deborah Bissell

DEBORAH'S EASY & DELICIOUS WHEAT ROLLS

MAKES 12 TO 16 ROLLS

2 tablespoons yeast
1 cup warm water
pinch sugar
4 cups warm milk
1 cup sugar (or ½ cup honey)
½ cup oil
4 teaspoons salt
4 eggs
14 cups flour (whole wheat, white or combination of both)

Dissolve yeast and pinch of sugar in warm water. Combine the
warm milk, sugar, oil, and salt in a large bowl with 6 cups flour;
beat well. Beat in yeast mixture and 4 eggs. Stirring by hand,
gradually add in 8 more cups of flour. It will be a soft dough.
Spray top with Pam, cover and let dough rise until double in size.
Punch down and separate into 4 parts. Roll one part
into a 12 inch circle. Brush dough with melted butter.
Take a pizza cutter and cut into pie sections (12 to 16 pieces).
Start at large end and roll up. (Repeat for other three parts
of dough or vary as below.) Let them rise for 20 minutes
on a greased cookie sheet. Bake at 350 for 12-15 minutes
or until lightly browned.

VARIATION: Cinnamon rolls. Roll the section into
a rectangle shape. Spread with melted butter.
Sprinkle with cinnamon and sugar. Roll up long ways.
Cut into 1 inch thick sections and place on a greased cookie
sheet. Let them rise for 20 minutes.
Bake at 350 for 15-20 minutes or until lightly browned.

Grand-daughter, Deborah Bissell

Helpful Hints

I have found over the years,
if we can have a positive attitude,
and think of what we are doing
as a mini adventure, life can be
pleasurable and fruitful.

When we embark on any adventure
we should be as well-prepared as
possible. I hope these few hints
will help you to be prepared,
to have a little fun along the way,
and happy and content
at the end of each of your
culinary journeys.

Bea

I measure all ingredients and put them in small bowls before
I begin to stir up cakes. I think it avoids mistakes in measuring.

Always double-check your oven to be sure you have placed the
racks properly and that your temperature is set correctly for
what you are planning to bake.

A good set of measuring spoons and measuring cups are
most important for success in the kitchen.

Try to have the proper size pans for your various recipes.

Don't be afraid to experiment with spices and flavorings.
Sometimes a little more of this and a little less of that, may
suit your family's taste better.

When trying a new recipe, remember, if at first you don't
succeed, and so on.

A little, flour, an egg or two, a little shortening, a bit of leavening,
and flavoring, and, "Eureka", a minor miracle!

Remember, when you are preparing a meal, a little
Tender Loving Care is your most important ingredient.

Remember practice can make perfect.

"When your left hand doesn't know what the right hand is doing,"
you may be in deep trouble in the kitchen.

Good company, good music, good food, good times.

Don't cry over spilled milk, unless it's the last you have,
and all the rest of your cake ingredients are already mixed.

Your old recipes are like old friends, they rarely let you down.

Use the best brands, brands you are used to, sometimes a penny
saved is not necessarily a penny earned.

Complicated recipes are not always your best choice, particularly
if you are rushed. Too many opportunities for error.

If a recipe doesn't turn out the way you hoped, remember
tomorrow is another day.

If you are disappointed at the out-come of a recipe, just
ask yourself how many times does a golfer hit that little ball
before he makes "a hole in one".

Cooking is like piano lessons, how many lessons before you
become a concert pianist.

"What's sauce for the goose, is sauce for the gander,"
it generally just takes a little more for the gander.

"A tisket, a tasket, off to market I go with my big yellow basket."
Company coming.

Always remember the proof of the pudding is in the eating,
try always to make it good.

I use Pillsbury's Best flour for pies, biscuits and all recipes
which call for all-purpose flour.

I use Soft-a-Silk cake flour for cakes and some cookies.

I use only Calumet baking powder.

I never, ever use any mayonnaise other than Hellman's.

I use only Domino sugar, granulated, confectioners
and brown sugar.

I use Gold Medal Wondra flour to make my rolls.

Old Mother Hubbard went to the cupboard
to get her poor doggie a bone.
But when she got there, the cupboard was bare so she said,
"I guess I'll just have to bake him one."
And so dog biscuits were born .

Buy the freshest vegetables and fruits possible.
Their shelf life is limited.

Being a cheerful cook is its own reward.

Try always to allow yourself a little extra time to prepare a meal.
It may avoid a disaster.

We'll never know how many hidden talents we have,
until we explore new endeavors.

To family and friends there's nothing like the aroma of
something good cooking in your kitchen.

Try to cook at lower temperatures when cooking
on the stovetop. It is more economical and in most cases
produces a better tasting product.

Check the temperature in your refrigerator now and then;
especially when you place large quantities of meats
and vegetables in at one time.

Being a cheerful cook is it's own special reward.

As long as your children live, they will remember the little
special treats you made for them.

Think of preparing a meal as a gift to those you love.

Knowing we have done our best, is in itself compensating.

If at first you don't succeed, you have a perfectly good reason
to try again.

Don't fret if you make a few mistakes, they are part of
life's great learning aids.

We learn by doing, and doing, and doing, and doing.

"People tend to save the best for last", try to make our
desserts a happy ending to a good meal.

And then we have what they call "a baker's dozen."
I guess that just depends on the baker.

A good hot, bowl of soup on a cold winter's night; *S'wonderful.*

Do you remember your first birthday cake still?

There's nothing quite like that first red ripe tomato
from your very own garden.

A bowl of fresh, sliced, ripe peaches and ice cream
on a sultry August evening,...yum...yum.

A picnic table, laden with home fried chicken,
macaroni and cheese, fresh roasting ears of corn,
luscious sliced red ripe tomatoes, fresh apple pie and
home made ice cream, family and friends seated at the table
laughing and talking makes a beautiful memory.

Any meal prepared with love, will taste just a little bit better
to your family.

To be a good cook you need to want to please.

Do you remember the first home-cooked meal you
served your new husband as a bride. It might be fun
to repeat it again.

Lucky the cook who has her own little herb garden. With fresh
herbs, what fantastic dishes she can prepare.

Remember the days your mother or grand-mother would spend
sometimes weeks, preparing cookies and other goodies
for the holidays.

Approach preparing a meal, as an opportunity to be creative.

Today's cooks are so fortunate; not too long ago, we grew, canned, dried or froze all our own vegetables, fruits, meats and fowl.

Fifty years ago, we could never have imagined how different and streamlined food preparation is now.

I am convinced some recipes were the result of minor mistakes in seasonings, ingredients or procedures.

When assembling a recipe you find you haven't a certain ingredient, try to substitute another ingredient that may be compatible.

The blending of ingredients can be so important, especially in some recipes.

"An apple a day keeps the doctor away" don't bet on it if he smells them baking.

When is a cake not a cake, when they say it's "a work of art."

"Jack Spratt could eat no fat, his wife could eat no lean," but they solved their problem just fine.

Little Jack Horner sat in a corner eating his Christmas pie. Remember what happened?

"Peas porridge hot, peas porridge cold, peas porridge in the pot nine days old," it doesn't say too much for the cook.

"To market to market, to buy a fat pig." What happened to 80% lean?

Garnishes can add so much to the simplest dishes.

Planning a meal well ahead, selecting the right platters
and bowls for the foods you are serving, relieves a lot of stress;
particularly when you are having guests.

A sprig of parsley, a dash of paprika, a twist of lemon,
a sprinkle of nuts, anything to add a little eye appeal
will make the dish more interesting.

Try not to settle family arguments at the dinner table.
Light pleasant conversation is the key to "a happy meal"

Food preparation is an opportunity for self expression,
whether in menu planning, preparation or presentation.

Good cooking is truly an art and so it has been dubbed a
"Culinary Art!"

Most of us will spend a life-time "cooking." There will always be
new ideas, new recipes, new ways in preparation, but let us not
say, "off with the old, on with the new," there will always
be some of the old ideas that will survive or be revised.

The milk of "human kindness" should be in our menu everyday.

"Jack and Jill went up the hill to fetch a pail of water,"
see how fortunate we modern cooks are.